Penguin Critical Studies

Shakespeare: Text into Performance

Peter Reynolds lectures in drama and theatre studies at the Roehampton Institute. He was trained as an actor at the Central School of Speech and Drama and at the London Academy of Music and Dramatic Art (LAMDA). He subsequently worked in the theatre in Britain and America before going to Sussex University to read English. His publications include *Critical Studies: As You Like It* (Penguin Books, 1988) and *Practical Approaches to Teaching Shakespeare*.

Penguin Critical Studies
Advisory Editor: Bryan Loughrey

Shakespeare: Text into Performance

Peter Reynolds

Penguin Books

PENGUIN BOOKS

Published by the Penguin Group
Penguin Books Ltd, 27 Wrights Lane, London W8 5TZ, England
Penguin Books USA Inc., 375 Hudson Street, New York, New York 10014, USA
Penguin Books Australia Ltd, Ringwood, Victoria, Australia
Penguin Books Canada Ltd, 10 Alcorn Avenue, Ontario, Canada M4V 3B2
Penguin Books (NZ) Ltd, 182–190 Wairau Road, Auckland 10, New Zealand

Penguin Books Ltd, Registered Offices: Harmondsworth, Middlesex, England

First published 1991
10 9 8 7 6 5 4 3 2 1

Filmset in 9/11 pt Monophoto Times New Roman
Printed in England by Clay's Ltd, St Ives plc

For Kim

Contents

Contents

Acknowledgements and Bibliographical Note

I am grateful to the Principal and Governors of the Froebel Institute College for their generosity and support during the writing and rewriting of this book. The extensive changes I have made to the original edition (*Drama: Text into Performance*, Penguin Books, 1986), have also been made possible through the continued support and stimulus I have received from my students on the 'Shakespeare's Texts in Modern Contexts' course at the Roehampton Institute. My greatest debt however is to my wife, Kimberley Reynolds, whose love and support, not to mention her editorial tact and skill, are invaluable to me.

All extracts from Shakespeare are taken from the New Penguin Shakespeare except for the passage from *Cymbeline* on p. 74 which is taken from *William Shakespeare: The Complete Works* (Penguin Books, 1969).

Introduction

Despite being born in obscurity over 400 years ago, remaining in it for most of his life, and leaving almost no documentary evidence of his existence, the name and reputation of William Shakespeare towers over much of Western culture like a colossus. In the British theatre today, his plays are performed with greater frequency than those of any other dramatist, living or dead. The recent implementation of a national curriculum in all English state schools has seen Shakespeare as the *only* named author in the English literature syllabus. There is a vast and ever-expanding Shakespeare industry in which the name 'Shakespeare' is used to sell products ranging from beer to banking, and also acts as a magnet attracting hundreds of thousands of tourists to the shrines of bardolatry in Stratford-upon-Avon, and, perhaps in the not too distant future, to the excavated remains of the Rose theatre, and the re-created Globe on the south bank of the Thames in London. People almost everywhere, in a huge variety of cultures, are influenced by the name of a long-dead poet and playwright, despite the fact that the majority of them will never have seen, and certainly never have read, a Shakespeare play. But simply because Shakespeare is very much in the public domain does not mean that what he wrote is accessible to everyone. The name and reputation of this great cultural monolith presents a considerable obstacle for the student of his plays.

In addition to Shakespeare's somewhat daunting reputation as a great artist, the common reader seeking to reclaim Shakespeare for himself or herself also has to face the considerable barrier erected by a beautiful, but now archaic language. But perhaps the highest hurdle that history has put in the way of the student seeking to come to terms with what Shakespeare produced, is the reputation his plays have for containing the seeds of permanent and lasting truths about people and society. Whether or not the plays of Shakespeare contain permanent truths about ourselves and our society is not of importance here. What is of concern is that too many students approach their study of the Bard with feelings of awe and wonder; feelings perhaps more appropriate and useful to a religious, rather than a cultural experience. If you begin your work with the assumption that what Shakespeare wrote contains lasting truths, then you are likely to spend a lot of time searching for them, and when they are 'revealed' (almost invariably by other people) it will be difficult for you, as an isolated individual, to question them. In my experience, too many prospective readers tend to be intimidated before they begin studying Shakespeare, and as a result, relinquish their own responses in order to have them safely mediated through the works of Shakespearean authorities; not just academics, but also organizations such as the BBC and the Royal Shakespeare Company (RSC).

Shakespeare criticism and scholarship plays a valuable role in broadening and deepening our appreciation and understanding of Shakespeare, especially when it places him in his own historical and social context.

The generally innovative and exciting productions of Shakespeare's plays consistently coming from the RSC can provide an enormously challenging and important stimulus to the critical debate about what Shakespeare means to a modern society. But students of any age, and at any level, need to be encouraged to think for themselves, and the name and reputation of Shakespeare compounds their difficulty in doing this. Although *Shakespeare: Text into Performance* does not seek in any way to challenge Shakespeare's reputation as a great dramatist, it is intended to encourage a more genuinely independent approach to reading his plays. Independent, because first and foremost it approaches the texts as incomplete and partial without the added dimension of performance, real or imagined.

When a prospective reader walks into a bookshop, or even into a local library, he or she usually has to look quite hard to find the shelf, or portion of a shelf, that holds a selection of plays. Novels, on the other hand, seem to be everywhere – even the local supermarket will offer a selection, albeit generally of a sensational and often lurid nature. Hardly anybody, it seems, wants to buy or read plays of whatever kind, even the plays of Shakespeare. Were it not for their presence on GCSE and A level syllabuses, and the reading lists of humanities degree courses, most would probably not get printed in anything like the numbers of editions that now abound. By contrast, there is a tolerably healthy market in Britain and America for those who wish to see performances of Shakespeare's plays in the theatre. It appears that there is an *audience* for his work, but, outside schools and academia, not much of a *readership*. It is highly unlikely that this book will have such a dramatic effect on the market for the printed texts of Shakespeare's plays, that supermarket managers around the land will be rushing to fill their shelves in order to satisfy the awakened appetite of customers now eager to consume them. However, I do covet the modest

hope that readers of this book will be encouraged and helped in recognizing that reading plays, especially those of Shakespeare, is not necessarily
a poor substitute to seeing them. It can be a tremendously exciting and
enjoyable experience, and anyone who seriously wants to consider
theatrical performance – from whatever point of view – must first be
able to rehearse imaginatively the translation of ideas from page to
stage.

It is impossible to pick up a copy of a Shakespeare play and read it
without, on some level, re-creating it in the theatre of the mind's eye.
This appears as a *natural* and instinctive response, and as such is very
often taken for granted and certainly not subjected to critical scrutiny.
But there is nothing *natural* about it. Despite what one of Shakespeare's
characters alleged, the imagination does not 'body forth the forms of
things unknown' (THESEUS, *A Midsummer Night's Dream*, V, i, lines
14–15). What is seen on the stage of the mind's eye is constructed by
many different factors, both social and cultural. In particular, the imaginary re-enactment of a play-text is controlled, or heavily influenced
by, our own, often subconscious adherence to the dominant theatrical
conventions of staging plays in the late twentieth century. Such conventions seem natural enough now, and are often taken for granted, but
they may be entirely inappropriate to the conventions of staging that
governed the historical genesis of the play, especially if that play
happens to have been written by Shakespeare.

Twentieth-century Western theatre is dominated by illusionist conventions of staging, and by an acting style that relies heavily on naturalistic
technique. This is especially so in television and film, the media through
which many people have their first, and sometimes only, experience of
Shakespeare in performance. But Shakespeare wrote for a very different
kind of theatre, one that did not, and could not, attempt to create any
illusion of reality in the staging of its plays. Far from pretending that
the audience are not actually there in the auditorium watching them,
Elizabethan actors often directly addressed that audience, both in character, and as themselves. Boys enacted women's roles, and the entire
location of the action was signalled by the words and gestures of the
actors, not by the stage designer, which was then a non-existent role.

This book aims to enrich and enliven the process of reading Shakespeare's plays by encouraging the reader to be more aware and informed
about current and historical theatrical conventions, Shakespeare's stage-
craft and the decisions that are taken (often unconsciously) when dramatic literature is transformed imaginatively into a theatrical event. In
order to develop a critical perspective on what is happening in the mind

during the process of reading plays, it is necessary to look at how a play is constructed in rehearsal and performance, and by whom. Above all, the reader needs to acknowledge that although our culture elevates the creativity of an individual man – William Shakespeare – his work was, and still is, totally inseparable from the collective and collaborative creative process that reproduces it. In remaking Shakespeare in the theatre, many people are involved in constructing and reconstructing new meanings. This sometimes proves difficult to accept in an age which tends to regard performances of Shakespeare as ephemeral (especially if they are dubbed 'gimmicky') in contrast to what are perceived to be the more lasting qualities of a printed text created by one individual and read by another. However, reading a play by Shakespeare (or anyone else) ought to reflect the excitement of the collaborative process that is necessary in order to reproduce it. The reader who approaches the text in this way will need to accept as necessary *and legitimate* the need to take interpretative decisions requiring evaluative risks. The reader of any text completes that text by the act of reading it, but it is especially important that the reader of Shakespeare's plays takes on board the simple idea, but one with great implications, that the printed text of *any* play is incomplete and partial without the added dimension of performance, be it imagined or practically realized.

The fact that this is not a new idea does not necessarily make it any easier to accept, let alone to act upon. The old, nineteenth-century prejudices that considered Shakespeare to be best left to the quiet intimacy of a gentleman's study – far removed from the popular vulgarity of theatre audiences and the tendency towards self-aggrandizement of actor-managers – have gradually declined, but they have not disappeared. Nevertheless, over the last two decades there has been a tremendous growth in critical literature acknowledging that plays, including the plays of Shakespeare, need to be considered in the context of performance. Today, actors and directors are far more likely than they would have been in the past to be invited by scholars to articulate their ideas about Shakespeare, not only on the stage, but also on the page. Books such as Carol Rutter's *Clamorous Voices: Shakespeare's Women Today* (interviews with five leading actresses about playing in Shakespeare), and the collected thoughts of contemporary *Players of Shakespeare* (Vol. I edited by Brockbank; Vol. II edited by Jackson and Smallwood), have provided a valuable resource for anyone interested in the theatre, and especially in Shakespeare. The old apartheid that divided academic and theatrical life has begun to disappear, and many new insights and enhanced understandings have been developed as a consequence.

What emerges from reading this new literature on theatrical production is that neither actors, directors nor designers approach a play in the same way. But that they are all engaged in making statements about the text, seeking all the time to make new meanings from, in the case of Shakespeare, very familiar material. As Jonathan Miller, erstwhile director of London's Old Vic theatre and a vastly experienced director of Shakespeare, has said, 'One of the reasons why Shakespeare continues to be performed is not that there *is* a central realizable intention in each play that we still continue to value, but because we are still looking for the possibility of unforeseen meanings' (*Subsequent Performances*, p. 35). To engage in the search for unforeseen meanings as a *reader* of plays, requires an alliance of the intellect and imagination in order to effect the lifting of a play off the page and into imaginary theatrical life. The reader has to *make it happen.* He or she must employ intellectual skills to open up ideas in the printed text of a play that seem significant, and then take delight in using the imagination to create theatrical forms that will succeed in animating those ideas. It does not matter if the unforeseen meanings have, in fact, been seen many times before by others. What does matter is that the reader takes some of the responsibility for *making* meanings, and, as a result, discovers the delight in the process of creation and discovery that is the essence of theatre, and which an active approach engenders.

This book is not intended as a guide on how to produce Shakespeare's plays, or those of any other dramatist, but it is a book which seeks to make the reader aware and reassured that Shakespeare's text is *a* text, and not *the* text; it is the starting-point, and serves as a blueprint for necessary further action. Actors, directors, designers and audiences all make their own texts from what a dramatist has given them, but what they make is *not* the same thing as what has been printed, although the printed text is where the process of interpretation usually starts.

I want to call this approach to reading Shakespeare 'active' reading, because for many people the act of reading itself is regarded as a solitary business, and essentially passive in nature. Theatre, on the other hand, seems more lively, and is attractive to many students because it is a shared experience involving an active relationship between audience and performers. The kind of active reading I am proposing is also a kind of shared experience, and certainly demands the opposite of a passive response. It requires the reader to acknowledge and celebrate the fact that meanings in performances are collectively constructed, and to participate fully and consciously in taking decisions concerning the imaginative re-enactment of Shakespeare. But he or she must also

know the argument which forms the base from which those interpretative decisions have sprung, and the relationship it has to what
is printed. There is a well-known anecdote concerning the late Sir
Laurence Olivier when, as the director of the National Theatre, he was
playing the lead role in Shakespeare's *Othello* at the Old Vic theatre in
London. After one evening's stupendous performance, Olivier was con-
gratulated by members of the cast who told him how brilliant his
performance had been. They were disconcerted to find the knight angry
rather than pleased; angry because he knew it had been good, but
didn't know how or why. Indeed, it is often the case that an actor gives
a performance which strikes critics as revelatory without knowing consciously why, or even how, the effect was achieved – in the end, it really
doesn't matter. In fact, too much thinking and analysing may be a
barrier for some actors, preventing them from giving the kind of performance they feel a role requires. But, for a student of dramatic literature
it is not enough to *feel* something is right; he or she must be able to
argue for it, and say how it is to be achieved. In order to do this the
active reader must recognize, and then attempt to organize the huge
variety of visual and oral signs that are contained within the body of
the modern, printed edition of a Shakespeare play, and which, during
the act of reading, are consciously and subliminally at work, making an
imaginary performance in the theatre of the mind's eye. In the process
of thus constructing an imaginary performance text, the active reader
must accept that no single sign, or generator of that sign – be it the
gesture of an actor at a particular moment, the way a line of spoken
text is inflected, or a colour used significantly in a designer's setting – is
the text, but that any performance text is a combination – a blend – of
many different signs and signals emanating from different sources.

In reading a play on the page, the words spoken by the actors seem
the most important sign of what the play means, but in performance
words are only one of many ways in which meaning is constructed. It is
the collective expression of the myriad signs and signals that comprises
the play in performance, and each performance is different from the
previous one. Indeed, witnesses of a performance see the text in their
own way, and not that of their neighbours. That this is so becomes
evident from even the most cursory glance at dramatic criticism, let
alone from the greatly contrasting discussions of what took place, and
its significance, that occur whenever a lively group of people watch the,
purportedly, same performance of a play. Just as all the participants in
a performance text, and all the members of an audience witnessing it,
have to make their own texts, so the active reader has to make his or

hers, and that text will be the result of the synthesis created after juggling with the different, but complementary textual statements that comprise the transition from text into performance. Therefore the active reader has to develop a multi-focused approach to the text, and certainly cannot simply concentrate on spoken dialogue. It is a challenging task, but one which greatly enhances the pleasure of reading, watching and in any way encountering Shakespeare's plays.

The Printed Text

In order to begin to develop a multi-focused approach to reading Shakespeare as a dramatist, it is not necessary to design, direct or act in his plays, although some of you may well do so. However, your ultimate objective of being able to translate what is given on the printed page into an imaginative and effective theatrical event, will only be achieved through familiarity with what Shakespeare wrote for actors to speak. Whether it is in the classroom or in the rehearsal-room, work towards a text-into-performance must begin with very close scrutiny of the dramatist's text as it has been printed and published. As this is the beginning of this book, and of our scrutiny of the dramatic texts of Shakespeare, it is as well to emphasize the importance of reading and rereading that text *before* any collective decisions are negotiated, and the rehearsal debate begun. It is difficult for many people to pick up a Shakespeare play and read it 'cold'. There are ways of assisting the reader in this process, some of which are referred to at the end of this book, but you cannot begin to construct a real or imaginary performance text out of a printed one unless, and until, you have done the necessary preparation. Whatever creative ideas may subsequently emerge as the result of your debates with yourself, or others, over what you come to define as the texts of actor, director and designer, you must be able to argue for their authority from the basis of a sound knowledge of the starting-point for all subsequent textual statements: Shakespeare's text. Your task is to get to know that text, and to develop enough confidence to enable you to release some of its latent potential for dramatic expression through the exercise of your *informed* imagination.

What follows in this chapter, and indeed in the rest of the book, is not a complete and exhaustive study of the complexities of making an imaginary performance text out of a printed one. What I shall concentrate on is what I have found useful and interesting in my own study of text-into-performance, and what I feel is too often neglected when the emphasis on the study of plays is literary as opposed to dramatic.

Textual Authority

In contemporary culture we are encouraged to trust and value the printed word. A performance of a play is an ephemeral thing, changing from day to day and all too soon forgotten, but a play committed to print seems altogether more permanent and to carry with it an aura of authority. But that authority, seen as a basis for interpretation, is not always what it seems. This is particularly true in the case of plays by Shakespeare and his contemporaries. When you begin to study his work, remember that *no* manuscripts of Shakespeare's plays survive. Indeed, there are very few manuscripts available to scholars (or anyone else) of plays of the Elizabethan and Jacobean period. In a sense, this chapter could more accurately be entitled 'The Editor's Text', for, the modern editions of Shakespeare's plays that you are likely to read and study, and indeed the editions used as a basis for making modern texts into performances in our theatres, have been put together by editors from early (sixteenth and seventeenth century) printed versions of the plays, published in small editions after the play itself had ceased to be regularly performed. In these quarto or folio editions the text is not always divided into acts and scenes, and when it is, the work, together with the punctuation, spelling and stage directions, is that of the first compositors who set the type from a manuscript probably supplied by the theatre. Also, some of the earliest printed versions of the same Shakespeare play differ, sometimes quite significantly, in the text that they print. The question then arises as to which of the different versions is the 'correct' one. Of course the answer is that there is *no definitive edition*: what may have become known as, for example, *the* generally accepted text of *Hamlet*, has been reconstructed by generations of scholars from several of the earliest printed editions of the play.

Although there are some notable exceptions such as Ben Jonson, Shakespeare, like many other dramatists of the period, seems to have taken very little obvious interest in the publication of his work. This seems to have largely been for economic, rather than artistic reasons. Shakespeare was a member, a shareholder in fact, of a theatrical company which made its profits from selling performances, not from selling the rights to publication of plays. There was, in any case, no real protection of copyright for dramatists, and in order to prevent other groups of actors from stealing successful theatrical material, plays were only published after their immediate audience had been exhausted. The actors were only given a copy of their own parts (their roles); in part, this was in order to save time (copying) and money, but it was also a precautionary measure lest the temptation to sell the whole text to the highest bidder proved too much for them. This is, in fact, what some scholars suppose happened in the case of the so-called 'bad quarto' of

Hamlet. In this edition the text so widely differs from that of the other contemporary quartos and from the Folio text that some have suggested that it was a pirated version, made from notes taken by a member of the audience, and perhaps from information given by one or two of the minor players with less than perfect memories. Whatever its origins, we should remember that our modern printed text is, in a very real sense, only an approximation of what Shakespeare himself may, or may not, have originally written. What was set in type by the first printers of Shakespeare's work no doubt closely reflects what was written, and perhaps more closely than that, what was performed on the stage, but its authority is *not* absolute.

In the practice of Shakespeare's *theatre*, the authority of the written text was secondary to that of the spoken and the visual, and what was considered to be theatrically effective – what made people actually want to pay money to visit the theatre – was the paramount consideration of the actors and dramatist. Shakespeare was probably an actor as well as a writer, and his was a commercial theatre for which he, and his contemporaries, produced, as it were, working drawings – blueprints on which to base performances that could, and would, be adapted by the players as circumstances (meaning audiences) required. The Elizabethan theatre, unlike our own, did not possess a huge repertory of classic plays from the past. Almost all the plays shown on the public stages were being shown for the first time, this meant that there was tremendous pressure on dramatists such as Shakespeare to go on producing new plays, because audiences wanted, above all, to see new work. The players, or certainly the leading players like Burbage, would have had at least some freedom to make changes in what Shakespeare wrote, and to suggest (and demand) modifications and rewrites. In the high pressure circumstances under which Shakespeare worked, he probably welcomed and accepted this. Indeed, such a relationship between a dramatist and a theatre company is by no means unusual today. For example, when a company such as that at the Royal Court in London commissions a new play, its author does not come to the first rehearsal expecting it to be performed exactly as it has been written; the director and the actors working on the text in rehearsal, all contribute to its genesis. A good dramatist (and Shakespeare was a supremely good one) knows that good drama is generated as a result of a very close collaboration between performers, director and dramatist.

When these Comedies and Tragedies were presented on the stage, the actors omitted some scenes and passages (with the Author's consent) as occasion led

3

them; and when private friends desired a copy, they then (and justly too) transcribed what they acted.
(From the Stationers' Address (1647) to the collected plays of Beaumont and Fletcher.)

This is not to say that the relationship between a dramatist and a group of players is always without tension. Shakespeare was his company's resident dramatist; he knew the strengths and weaknesses of his company of players and wrote for them accordingly, but he couldn't always have been happy with what was done to his material on-stage, for, as Hamlet remarks to the players who visit Elsinore:

... let those that play your clowns speak no more than is set down for them. For there be of them that will themselves laugh to set on some quantity of barren spectators to laugh too, though in the meantime some necessary question of the play be then to be considered. That's villainous, and shows a most pitiful ambition in the fool that uses it.   (III, ii, lines 37–43)

What all this means for the active reader is that the modern printed edition of a Shakespeare play is not the *absolute* authority as to what should be permitted in the making of a performance text. Its authority, although considerable, is ultimately speculative and editorial rather than demonstrably authorial. This is important, and we do need to be reminded of it, if only because of the authority that the printed word currently commands in our culture.

Stage Directions

The closer we come to our own time, the greater the authority of the printed text becomes. Editions of modern plays are often published to coincide with their first performance; certainly playwrights today write to be read and to be seen. They can exercise total control over what is printed. Many attend the first and subsequent rehearsals of their plays, and influence, even if they cannot completely control, what is presented in performance as *their* work. The awareness of modern dramatists of the needs of the reader, and their desire to influence the production of their work in the theatre, sometimes leads to detailed instructions in the printed text as to how the performance text should be staged. The plays of Samuel Beckett cannot be negotiated by a reader simply by looking at what characters say. Beckett supplies copious stage directions that, if they are ignored, will totally distort the reader's perception. Directions such as these carry the unmistakable authority of their author, and it would be foolish and perverse to entirely disregard them. But, in the text that we have of a Shakespeare play, or indeed that of almost any other pre nineteenth century dramatist, the stage directions do *not* carry the same prescriptive weight.

When you begin to analyse Shakespeare's printed text, treat the stage directions with caution, as a guide rather than a rule as to how to read a scene. Remember that Shakespeare tailor-made his text to fit a small group of professional players whose work and ability he knew and understood. The group was small in number compared to today's large national companies, not through any natural reluctance of the general populace to thrust themselves upon the stage as performers, but because those who earned their living through what was an entirely commercial enterprise knew that the fewer they were in number, the greater the share of the proceeds of their art each could expect to receive. Therefore, with a permanent company of players totalling ten to twelve full-time professionals, the doubling and trebling of roles for most actors was a requirement of their employment. The cast list for *Hamlet*, for instance, lists no less than thirty-three named roles in addition to attendants, guards, sailors and so on. Of course, many of the smaller roles, particularly those not required to speak, would have been played by the so-called 'hired men', the Elizabethan equivalent of today's extras or spear carriers. But all the main roles would have been covered by the men of the permanent company; thus, the two actors who open *Hamlet* as Barnardo and Francisco are equally likely to have ended it as Osrick and Fortinbras, having played First Player and Ophelia in between. When you see a printed list of characters who are to appear in a scene, remember that the absence of a particular character may originally have been for *practical* (the actor was required for another role), rather than interpretative reasons. Thus in Act I, scene ii of *Hamlet* the directions state:

Flourish
   Enter Claudius, King of Denmark, Gertrude the Queen, and the Council, including Polonius with his son Laertes, Hamlet, Voltemand, Cornelius, and attendants

A pretty full list, but is it complete? Could or should any other character be present? I suggest that it is perfectly legitimate for you, the active reader, to suggest *and argue* for the presence in this scene of Ophelia. After all, her father and brother are both present. Of course she is given no words to speak but, as we will see later, silent characters are often amongst the most visually eloquent of those on stage. Alternatively, you could argue that her absence indicates the low status of women in this court, especially when the business of State is being transacted. Although Gertrude is present, it is in her role as Queen rather than as a woman and the wife of Claudius. My point is simply that Shakespeare's stage directions are not sacrosanct; you must judge for yourself their appropriateness and not let the circumstances of the original playing conditions unnecessarily limit your freedom to reinterpret your text-into-performance. The only absolutely reliable stage directions in Shakespeare are those that come from the text spoken by the actors. For instance in the first scene of *Hamlet*:

BARNARDO

> Sit down awhile,
> And let us once again assail your ears,
> That are so fortified against our story,
> What we have two nights seen.
>
> (lines 30–33)

and to which the reply is:

HORATIO

> Well, sit we down,
> And let us hear Barnardo speak of this.
>
> (line 34)

It is quite obvious what should happen in performance, and you would have to begin to *adapt* the text, as opposed to interpreting it, if you wanted to see things differently.

In addition to stage directions that are not always clear or complete, Shakespeare also leaves the active reader with a good deal of other work to do if he or she is to make a performance text out of a printed one. Shakespeare does not spell out to the reader, actor, director, designer or anyone else, *exactly* how his text should be made into a performance, but he has left a lot of clues in the text that need to be investigated. In order to demonstrate the process of reading *Shakespeare: Text into Performance*, I want to look in detail at the beginning of one of his most famous plays. The opening stage directions in *Hamlet* are minimal, but if we patiently work through the modern, printed text we will begin to see that there are clues within it as to possible presentational strategies. What we will certainly see is the number and nature of the interpretative decisions – indeed the risks – that need to be taken in order that you, as an active reader, make a unique, imaginative, theatrical event out of a piece of, probably, very familiar dramatic literature.

Do please read or reread the opening scene before you go on, otherwise what follows below will not mean anything to you. Remember that what I am offering you is *my* imaginary creation of this text-into-performance, based on evidence I can find in the printed text. It has no particular merit or status, and it is certainly not *the* text. It becomes *a* text by drawing upon a range of textual statements that I find significant. Adopt its method, its way of working, but do not necessarily adopt its conclusions.

Enter Francisco and Barnardo, two sentinels   I.i

BARNARDO Who's there?

FRANCISCO Nay, answer me. Stand and unfold yourself.

BARNARDO Long live the King!

FRANCISCO Barnardo?

BARNARDO He.

FRANCISCO
  You come most carefully upon your hour.

BARNARDO
  'Tis now struck twelve. Get thee to bed, Francisco.

FRANCISCO
  For this relief much thanks. 'Tis bitter cold,
  And I am sick at heart.

BARNARDO
  Have you had quiet guard?

FRANCISCO   Not a mouse stirring.   10

BARNARDO
  Well, good night.
  If you do meet Horatio and Marcellus,
  The rivals of my watch, bid them make haste.

    Enter Horatio and Marcellus

FRANCISCO
  I think I hear them. Stand ho! Who is there?

HORATIO
  Friends to this ground.

MARCELLUS   And liegemen to the Dane.

FRANCISCO
  Give you good night.

MARCELLUS   O, farewell, honest soldier.
  Who hath relieved you?

FRANCISCO   Barnardo hath my place.
  Give you good night.   *Exit*

MARCELLUS   Holla, Barnardo!

BARNARDO   Say –
  What, is Horatio there?

HORATIO   A piece of him.

BARNARDO
  Welcome, Horatio. Welcome, good Marcellus.   20

MARCELLUS
  What, has this thing appeared again tonight?

BARNARDO
  I have seen nothing.

MARCELLUS
  Horatio says 'tis but our fantasy,
  And will not let belief take hold of him
  Touching this dreaded sight twice seen of us.
  Therefore I have entreated him along
  With us to watch the minutes of this night,
  That, if again this apparition come,
  He may approve our eyes and speak to it.

HORATIO
  Tush, tush, 'twill not appear.

BARNARDO   Sit down awhile,   30
  And let us once again assail your ears,
  That are so fortified against our story,
  What we have two nights seen.

HORATIO   Well, sit we down,
  And let us hear Barnardo speak of this.

BARNARDO
  Last night of all,
  When yond same star that's westward from the pole
  Had made his course t'illume that part of heaven
  Where now it burns, Marcellus and myself,
  The bell then beating one –
       Enter the Ghost

MARCELLUS
  Peace, break thee off. Look where it comes again.   40

BARNARDO
  In the same figure like the King that's dead.

MARCELLUS
  Thou art a scholar. Speak to it, Horatio.

BARNARDO
  Looks 'a not like the King? Mark it, Horatio.

HORATIO
  Most like. It harrows me with fear and wonder.

BARNARDO
  It would be spoke to.

MARCELLUS   Speak to it, Horatio.

HORATIO
  What art thou that usurpest this time of night,
  Together with that fair and warlike form
  In which the majesty of buried Denmark
  Did sometimes march? By heaven I charge thee, speak.

MARCELLUS
  It is offended.
BARNARDO   See, it stalks away.   50
HORATIO
  Stay. Speak, speak. I charge thee, speak.   *Exit the Ghost*
MARCELLUS
  'Tis gone and will not answer.
BARNARDO
  How now, Horatio? You tremble and look pale.
  Is not this something more than fantasy?
  What think you on't?
HORATIO
  Before my God, I might not this believe
  Without the sensible and true avouch
  Of mine own eyes.
MARCELLUS   Is it not like the King?
HORATIO
  As thou art to thyself.
  Such was the very armour he had on   60
  When he the ambitious Norway combated.
  So frowned he once when, in an angry parle,
  He smote the sledded poleaxe on the ice.
  'Tis strange.
MARCELLUS
  Thus twice before, and jump at this dead hour,
  With martial stalk hath he gone by our watch.
HORATIO
  In what particular thought to work I know not.
  But, in the gross and scope of mine opinion,
  This bodes some strange eruption to our state.
MARCELLUS
  Good now, sit down, and tell me he that knows   70
  Why this same strict and most observant watch
  So nightly toils the subject of the land,
  And why such daily cast of brazen cannon
  And foreign mart for implements of war,
  Why such impress of shipwrights, whose sore task
  Does not divide the Sunday from the week.
  What might be toward that this sweaty haste
  Doth make the night joint-labourer with the day?
  Who is't that can inform me?
HORATIO   That can I.
  At least the whisper goes so. Our last King,   80
  Whose image even but now appeared to us,
  Was, as you know, by Fortinbras of Norway,

9

Thereto pricked on by a most emulate pride,
Dared to the combat; in which our valiant Hamlet –
For so this side of our known world esteemed him –
Did slay this Fortinbras; who, by a sealed compact
Well ratified by law and heraldry,
Did forfeit, with his life, all these his lands
Which he stood seised of, to the conqueror;
Against the which a moiety competent   90
Was gagèd by our King, which had returned
To the inheritance of Fortinbras,
Had he been vanquisher, as, by the same covenant
And carriage of the article designed,
His fell to Hamlet. Now, sir, young Fortinbras,
Of unimprovèd mettle hot and full,
Hath in the skirts of Norway here and there
Sharked up a list of lawless resolutes
For food and diet to some enterprise
That hath a stomach in't; which is no other,   100
As it doth well appear unto our state,
But to recover of us by strong hand
And terms compulsatory those foresaid lands
So by his father lost. And this, I take it,
Is the main motive of our preparations,
The source of this our watch, and the chief head
Of this posthaste and romage in the land.

BARNARDO

I think it be no other but e'en so.
Well may it sort that this portentous figure
Comes armèd through our watch so like the King   110
That was and is the question of these wars.

HORATIO

A mote it is to trouble the mind's eye.
In the most high and palmy state of Rome,
A little ere the mightiest Julius fell,
The graves stood tenantless and the sheeted dead
Did squeak and gibber in the Roman streets –
As stars with trains of fire and dews of blood,
Disasters in the sun; and the moist star
Upon whose influence Neptune's empire stands
Was sick almost to Doomsday with eclipse.   120
And even the like precurse of feared events,
As harbingers preceding still the fates
And prologue to the omen coming on,
Have heaven and earth together demonstrated
Unto our climatures and countrymen.

Enter the Ghost
But soft, behold, lo where it comes again!
I'll cross it, though it blast me.
    He spreads his arms
Stay, illusion.
If thou hast any sound or use of voice,
Speak to me.   130
If there be any good thing to be done
That may to thee do ease and grace to me,
Speak to me.
If thou art privy to thy country's fate,
Which happily foreknowing may avoid,
O, speak!
Or if thou hast uphoarded in thy life
Extorted treasure in the womb of earth,
For which, they say, you spirits oft walk in death,
Speak of it.
    The cock crows
                Stay and speak. Stop it, Marcellus.   140

MARCELLUS
Shall I strike it with my partisan?

HORATIO
Do, if it will not stand.

BARNARDO   'Tis here.

HORATIO   'Tis here.   *Exit the Ghost*

MARCELLUS
'Tis gone.
We do it wrong, being so majestical,
To offer it the show of violence,
For it is as the air invulnerable,
And our vain blows malicious mockery.

BARNARDO
It was about to speak when the cock crew.

HORATIO
And then it started, like a guilty thing
Upon a fearful summons. I have heard   150
The cock, that is the trumpet to the morn,
Doth with his lofty and shrill-sounding throat
Awake the god of day, and at his warning,
Whether in sea or fire, in earth or air,
Th'extravagant and erring spirit hies
To his confine. And of the truth herein
This present object made probation.

MARCELLUS
It faded on the crowing of the cock.

Some say that ever 'gainst that season comes
Wherein our Saviour's birth is celebrated, 160
This bird of dawning singeth all night long.
And then, they say, no spirit dare stir abroad;
The nights are wholesome; then no planets strike;
No fairy takes; nor witch hath power to charm.
So hallowed and so gracious is that time.

HORATIO
So have I heard and do in part believe it.
But look, the morn in russet mantle clad
Walks o'er the dew of yon high eastward hill.
Break we our watch up. And by my advice
Let us impart what we have seen tonight 170
Unto young Hamlet. For, upon my life,
This spirit, dumb to us, will speak to him.
Do you consent we shall acquaint him with it,
As needful in our loves, fitting our duty?

MARCELLUS
Let's do't, I pray. And I this morning know
Where we shall find him most conveniently. *Exeunt*

Exposition, Mood, Atmosphere and Tension

At the beginning of the extract printed above, the following appears:

Enter Francisco and Barnardo, two sentinels

The reader gets little help from such sparse information. There is no geographical location indicator, and although it is just conceivable that in the original performance conditions, a member of the company held up a board with the location written on it, it is unlikely that such a device was employed because it would have slowed the pace of the action if it were repeated every time the location changed. In any case, as we shall see, once the spoken text begins it is not really required. That spoken text is where you will find the necessary information to enable you to imaginatively enact the scene. The exchange between Barnardo and Francisco clearly shows that Francisco is on guard alone *before* Barnardo's entrance. Most modern theatres either don't possess, or don't make use of, a curtain dividing the stage from the auditorium, and the open-air theatre where *Hamlet* was first staged certainly didn't have one. One of the first interpretative decisions confronting the active reader is, therefore, to decide how, and when, to get the actor playing Francisco on to the stage, and what he should do once he gets there. Let us, for the sake of argument, have him on-stage at his post from the minute the first members of the audience enter the auditorium. We have no curtain, and the actor is there for all to see. What then should he be doing? What signals is he transmitting to the audience by his presence? He is soon asked 'Have you had quiet guard?' (line 10), which tells you his soldierly role. You can discover clues as to how to enact that guard from what is subsequently spoken. The dialogue reveals that it is night, cold, silent and still. Those are the key words that the actor playing Francisco needs to note in order to transmit the necessary atmosphere and mood at the opening of the play. He also has to convey whether or not his guard is ceremonial, or whether it is there because of a real need for security. Does he appear relaxed and bored, or tense and alert? Once you have considered his dramatic priorities as a performer, you must then decide how long he has to wait before the entrance of Barnardo. Silence in performance is a powerful force in creating unease and expectation amongst the audience. When is the silence and solitary nature of Francisco's watch broken by the noise of the oncoming Barnardo, and the ensuing opening *spoken* text of the performance?

The opening verbal exchange between the two actors seems quick and urgent in contrast to the silence that preceded it. They speak in short staccato sentences. Ask yourself why the play begins with a question; why does Barnardo need to ask 'Who's there?' Does he not recognize Francisco? In fact, both characters appear to require time to identify the other. This may indicate that in the original performance both men were to wear costumes that included a helmet with a visor which, when down, covered the face, perhaps to show that this guard is one in which it is necessary to be armed to the teeth. But, equally likely, Shakespeare is signalling to the audience that the scene is taking place at night, and the actors take time to see one another because they need to demonstrate to the audience in the open-air theatre in broad daylight, that on the stage it is 'dark'. Barnardo actually announces the time of day. To make it quite clear, he says not only that it has 'now struck twelve', but that it is time for Francisco to go to bed. The stress on time is important because not only is the action supposed to be taking place in darkness, but that darkness can also be metaphorical.

Entrances on to the stage are always dramatically significant. Not only do they introduce a new character, or give an opportunity for an actor who has previously been seen to re-establish his or her contact with the audience, they also change the *shape* and *pace* of the scene by the addition of their physical presence. The entrance of Horatio and

Marcellus is preceded by an off-stage noise indicated by Francisco's, 'I think I hear them'. This sound may be friendly or hostile, but it is evident from Francisco's challenge that he is not prepared to take any chances. We can, I think, assume that he moves towards the entry point of Horatio and Marcellus to make the challenge. The resulting confrontation mirrors the play's opening lines, and again reinforces the convention of darkness by the twice repeated 'Give you good night'.

The exit of Francisco leaves Barnardo alone with the two newcomers to the scene. Again he appears to have trouble recognizing them. Because they are some distance away (Francisco having halted their entrance up-stage), Barnardo needs to ask, 'Say – What, is Horatio there?' His uncertainty is only relieved when Horatio crosses the stage towards him with arm outstretched to offer his hand in greeting: 'A piece of him.'

Shakespeare stages this opening changing of the guard both to establish the time of day and to establish a mood of appropriate mystery and tension: things are both literally and metaphorically unclear. He also needs to suggest that in this place, at this time, there is an air of secrecy and even of conspiracy. Francisco *feels* that something is wrong, 'I am sick at heart', but he is not made privy to the secret shared between Barnardo, Marcellus and Horatio. When they are alone they begin to reveal what is causing the tension they, and the audience too, have experienced. Shakespeare is careful not to give too much away too quickly. Horatio does not ask about a ghost. He asks, far more effectively from the point of view of audience suspense, about 'this thing'. The audience then learn that something very strange has happened on previous occasions:

MARCELLUS
What, has this thing appeared *again* tonight?   (line 21, author's italics)

Slowly the audience are let into the secret, made a part of the conspiracy. When Marcellus speaks in response to Horatio's questions, 'this thing' becomes 'this dreaded sight twice seen of us'. At this point, for the audience, and indeed for Horatio, the phenomenon could be almost anything: a monster, a devil, a trick or a ghost. Whatever it is, the audience are presumably keen to find out more, and, at this point, Horatio acts as the representative of the audience by giving the kind of sceptical response which makes Barnardo reveal more of his story. He 'once again' attempts to convince Horatio (and the audience in the theatre) of the reality of what they have experienced.

The direction given by Shakespeare through Barnardo for the actors to adopt a particular *grouping* on stage is significant. They are to 'sit down' for two reasons. Firstly because in sitting they are in an attitude of listening to a story – an attitude in which the listeners are relatively relaxed and, literally, off guard. Secondly, the visual memory of the audience will later need to recall that soon-to-be-interrupted storytelling, and the act of sitting will be the visual key that triggers its recall.

As active readers we have to attempt to do more than simply note Shakespeare's stage directions, we have to *do* something as a result. In your (imagined) performance text you have to decide where the actors will sit and how. As you will see, your decisions are important. (I find it helpful to use a chess board and to label the chessmen as characters in the play and move them around on the 'stage'.) Let us say that the three are placed as far down-stage towards the audience as possible. Barnardo, the storyteller, is slightly up-stage of his listeners, and perhaps squatting on his haunches so that when he begins his tale he can direct what he says out across the actors and into the audience. Look for a moment at what he says: it is in the kind of language appropriate to a ghost story. Again there is the repetition of the convention of stage darkness: it is night, the stars are out. The probable striking of the bell by a stagehand serves both to remind the audience of time passing from the ''tis now struck twelve' of line 7 to one o'clock, and the cue to herald the entry of the Ghost. If the positioning of the actors is as I have suggested, then the audience (on-and off-stage) will see the actor representing the Ghost before the storyteller does. In a near-contemporary performance of Christopher Marlowe's *Doctor Faustus* in Exeter, a riot was narrowly avoided when members of the audience claimed that too many 'devils' had appeared on stage. It is not difficult, therefore, to anticipate a cry from the first audiences of *Hamlet* of 'Look out! Behind you!' – a cry that, unfortunately, we now only associate with children at pantomimes. For, however familiar the Elizabethans may have been with the appearance of ghosts in their theatre, they were certainly never completely sanguine or blasé about them. As Hamlet later remarks, in words that reflect the Elizabethan ambivalence and uncertainty concerning ghostly phenomena:

> ... The spirit that I have seen
> May be a devil, and the devil hath power
> T' assume a pleasing shape ...
> (II, ii, lines 596–8)

15

It is left to the actor playing Marcellus to let the audience make the connection between what they can now see, and the 'thing' they have previously heard of:

... Look where it comes *again*   (I, i, line 40, author's italics)

Barnardo then identifies the Ghost on behalf of the amazed audience as, 'In the same figure like the King that's dead'. Horatio's attempts to question the apparition are closely followed by the audience, who are by now as keen to know the answers as he is. But both are denied the satisfaction of an immediate explanation.

An obvious problem with the Ghost's entry comes when you begin to think what it should look like. When Jonathan Pryce played Hamlet a few years ago, in a production at London's Royal Court theatre directed by Richard Eyre, the Ghost was never actually seen on stage at all (the opening scene was cut entirely), but was represented by a disembodied male voice that seemed to come from within Hamlet himself.

Shakespeare's text gives us a clear idea of what *he* wanted to see. Horatio, in line 60, indicates how the Ghost should look when he refers to it as wearing armour. But, however you choose to represent old King Hamlet, what is important from the point of view of textual fidelity, is that the audience sees a man equipped to go to war: a king in military uniform, rather than a king in civilian clothes or robes of state. The text also offers a clue as to how the actor playing the Ghost shall perform, as Marcellus points out in line 66:

With *martial stalk* hath he gone by our watch.   (author's italics)

The Ghost does not remain on stage for very long. When it has gone, and the three actors are left alone again, there is a danger of the audience experiencing an anticlimax. The build-up to the Ghost's entrance created tension and a build-up of expectancy in the theatre, which is now in danger of becoming dissipated. Shakespeare counteracts this by a simple, but effective, device: he has Marcellus repeat Barnardo's original injunction to 'sit down'. This movement, especially if the grouping is similar or identical to the previous occasion, triggers the visual memory of the audience into recalling that the last time such an appeal was complied with it heralded the Ghost's appearance. When the action is completed, the audience watch and listen, expecting more immediate excitement. But, of course, they don't get what they expect. After their attention on the speaker is almost guaranteed, Shakespeare uses the focus of attention, not for a further episode in a ghost story, but for a very different, but equally important, kind of tale concerning politics and war.

The close attention of the audience to what Horatio is saying begins to be rewarded when the tone of his speech changes, signalling another shift in the mood and atmosphere of the performance. From line 80 to line 107 he recalls the events in the recent past that have led to the present situation of political confrontation. He speaks in the measured tones of an almost disinterested observer, using a calm and legalistic language full of references to 'inheritance', 'a sealed compact', and things 'Well ratified by law and heraldry'. But between lines 112 and 125 there is a radical shift as Horatio moves from contemplation of the dry facts behind the world's present political realities, to a thrilling story of the historical and mythical past. He uses a highly charged language which links the past and the present and speaks of the 'sheeted dead', of 'blood', 'Disasters' and of 'Doomsday'. It is possible that by having Horatio, the scholar and sceptic, use such theatrical language to describe the assassination of Julius Caesar, Shakespeare intended his audience to recall his own play *Julius Caesar*, performed, probably on the same stage, in the previous year. Certainly, what the change in Horatio's language does succeed in doing is to alter the atmosphere, and so prepare the audience for the second entry of the Ghost. To put it at its most basic, Shakespeare is trying to scare the audience.

The second entrance on to the stage by the Ghost turns out to be as inconclusive as the first. It fails to provide the audience, or Horatio, Barnardo and Marcellus, with the answers they are seeking: why is it there, and what does it want? Indeed, the whole of the play up to this point has raised the temperature of the action by posing a series of questions and then refusing to answer any of them. Something is most certainly very wrong, but everyone is in the literal and metaphorical dark about what it is. The emotions of the audience have been engaged by the performance text, and they have witnessed the beginning of, if not a horror story, then certainly a ghost story.

The departing Ghost triggers a sound effect (the crowing of a cock) which signals the impending arrival of day. But, the coming of dawn holds metaphorical significance. It heralds the prospect of some enlightenment of the extraordinary events the audience have witnessed and that have left them, and the players, in the dark. As Horatio says when the name of young Hamlet is first heard in the play that bears his name, 'This spirit [the Ghost], dumb to us, will speak to him' (line 172). What a wonderful preparation for the entrance of a leading actor this opening scene is. All that has happened has been an exercise in atmospheric preparation for Hamlet: he has been represented as the key that will unlock the mysteries of the subsequent action.

In looking at scene one in this kind of detail, we can see how the printed text of a Shakespeare play contains guidelines to how the reader can create an imagined performance, full of atmosphere and feeling. If we learn to read the signs, the act of reading can, like the theatrical experience itself, be a sensuous as well as a cerebral experience. I now want to continue to look at scene one of *Hamlet*, this time exploring how Shakespeare organizes the events on the stage in order to capture and then sustain the attention of the audience.

Dramatic Structure: Rhythm and Pace

The opening scene is constructed in a very clever but simple way in order to continually vary the shape and pace of the action. It can be divided into three distinct parts or movements. The opening section begins at the moment the audience begin to focus on Francisco as he enacts the guarding of the castle, and lasts until the Ghost has made his first exit. What distinguishes this movement from the other two is that the pace, once the spoken text commences, is uniformly quick. There is a real sense of urgency driving the initial exchanges between Francisco and Barnardo, marked by their use of short sentences. The initial pace is maintained by the rapid movements of the players on to and off the stage, and the appearance of the Ghost signals, literally, a frantic rush of movement to discover what it wants.

After the Ghost's exit the second movement begins. It is the longest of the three and ends with the second sighting of the Ghost. It is not only longer, but the pace is slower, more reflective and generally calm. It contains little action, but imparts a good deal of information about the state of Denmark. For most of the time, the actors assist the reflective, contemplative mood and slow the pace still further by remaining physically still. Like the audience, they are sitting and listening to what is being said. There are no entrances or exits to change the shape of the movement, and the short sentences of the first movement are replaced by much longer ones, and by speakers who speak without interruption for several minutes at a time instead of for a few seconds.

The third and final movement begins when the entry of the Ghost shatters the relative stability and calm of the second movement and causes, literally, the seated actors to rise and scatter across the stage. The pace is speeded up by Horatio's desperate repetition of 'Speak to me', and the attempts to strike the Ghost indicate fast movements by the players around the stage, as each actor moves from a sedentary position to an active, mobile one. After the Ghost has departed, the pace drops slightly, but the scene ends on a distinctly up-beat note. Marcellus, Barnardo and Horatio leave the stage displaying a sense of urgency and purpose. They want to get to Hamlet quickly and tell him what has happened for, 'This spirit, dumb to us, will speak to him' (line 172). The audience are left eagerly anticipating the sequel: it is on Prince Hamlet that their dramatic expectations are now clearly focused.

Stage Time

We have already noted that time is frequently referred to in Act One, scene one. The three-part structure of the scene is distinguished by the differences in time that each section presents. The audience experience the action first as highly compressed, then elongated, and then, in the last section, compressed again. A theatre audience cannot remain in a permanent state of high tension, certainly not for the whole of a performance, and therefore, in this opening scene, as well as throughout the play as a whole, the moments of high excitement are relatively brief and are followed by longer, calmer, episodes. The sense of movement and variety that is thus communicated is reflected in the changes in stage time (it moves from before midnight to just before dawn) that are also signalled. In the first movement stage time changes little, just over an hour in fact, from before midnight to midnight (''tis now struck twelve'), through to one o'clock (the Ghost last appeared when the bell struck one and presumably does so again). The mid-section covers, appropriately enough considering its much slower pace, a much longer period of stage time. It moves from shortly after one o'clock to just before the break of dawn: perhaps some four hours. The final movement takes us from that pre-dawn, signalled by the crowing of the cock ('the trumpet to the morn'), to Horatio's sighting of dawn itself:

> But look, the morn in russet mantle clad
> Walks o'er the dew of yon high eastward hill
> (lines 167–8)

and finally on to the very last line of the last section where Marcellus establishes that it is now morning:

> Let's do't, I pray. And I this morning know
> Where we shall find him most conveniently
> (lines 175–6)

19

This scene shows a tremendous compression of time, but it works in performance because of the different pace of the three-part structure.

We have explored how this first scene of *Hamlet* is constructed, how it plays on the emotions and the curiosity of the audience, how Shakespeare balances the focus of the audience between moments of tension and relaxation, between high drama and narrative exposition. Finally, I want to look not just at the first scene, but at the whole of the first act in terms of its dramatic organization and structure. Variety for the eye and the ear of the audience is, I think, one of the key factors in making Shakespeare such a potentially powerful and exciting force in performance. Let us look for a minute at the shape of the first act in terms of the varying number of actors on-stage at any one time. Scene one uses five; they make eight separate movements either on to or off the performance area. The movements can be broken down as follows: lines 1 to 14 use two actors; 15 to 18 use four; in 19 to 39 there are three; in 40 to 51 the number increases to four again; lines 52 to 125, the long mid-section of the scene, there are three again, who, on line 126 are joined by a fourth; and then from 142 until the close of the scene there are three actors again.

Scene one uses a small number of actors but constantly changes their number on-stage. Scene two (the council chamber), is in marked contrast to the first. It uses a much larger number of actors, *at least* eleven if you accept that the councillors and attendants total a minimum of four. The sparsely populated opening scene is replaced by a stage that now seems crowded. There are other notable differences from scene one. The actor who speaks first (in the role of Claudius), talks without interruption for thirty-nine lines, unlike the opening of the preceding scene when no actor spoke for more than a few lines at a time without interruption. But this second scene has, in common with the first, variety in its shape signalled by the changing number of actors on the stage. By line 42 the eleven are reduced to nine on the exit of Voltemand and Cornelius, and then, at line 128 there is a radical change in the shape of the scene, when all the actors except Hamlet leave the stage. The crowded stage, busy with the enactment of affairs of state, emphasizes Hamlet's isolated position, his lack of a meaningful role in the state of Denmark. Following Hamlet's soliloquy, the number of actors is raised to four by the entrance of Horatio, Barnardo and Marcellus. They remain together until line 254 when Hamlet is left alone again for the closing four lines of the scene. Thus in Act One, scene two the pattern of movement is: eleven actors down to nine; nine down to one; one up to four; and four down to one again.

Scene three begins with the entrance of two actors (Laertes and Ophelia) who, after fifty-two lines, are joined by a third (Polonius). Laertes leaves at line 87, leaving Ophelia and her father to end the scene after a further forty-nine lines. The scene is the simplest so far in terms of its structure and the number of actors used. But the fourth scene of the act is far more complex and mirrors much of the action of the first. It opens with the entry of three actors (Horatio, Marcellus and Hamlet) who, at line 38, are joined by a fourth (the Ghost). At line 68 Hamlet and the Ghost exit, leaving Horatio and Marcellus alone until the end of the scene.

The final scene of the first act opens with Hamlet and the Ghost entering together. They are on stage for ninety-one lines, the most extensive unbroken dialogue we have heard, until the Ghost exits leaving Hamlet alone. At line 112 his solitude is broken, first, by the sound of voices coming from off-stage, and then, at line 116, by the entry of Horatio and Marcellus. At line 149 the voice of the Ghost joins in intermittently until line 181. The rest of the scene is then played out by Hamlet, Horatio and Marcellus; the act ends as it began, with three actors holding the stage.

Hamlet is often thought of as a 'wordy' play, where the pace of the action is frequently interrupted in order to accommodate Hamlet's long, reflective soliloquies. But as the first act demonstrates, it is also a very active and dramatic text, full of movement and changes of pace. There must be literally dozens of exits and entrances of different characters in the opening act: really a tremendous amount of physical movement takes place – far more than in the majority of twentieth-century drama, which, by comparison, often seems static. Nothing remains still for long in *Hamlet*, neither the plot, the performers nor the location of the action. In Act One the latter moves from outside (scene one), to inside (scenes two and three) and back outside again (four and five). What takes place in those locations also changes, from events concerning the supernatural (in one, four and five), to the public and ceremonial life of the court (scene two), to the private domestic world exposed in the exchanges between members of the Polonius household in scene three.

Juxtaposing

Recognizing how Shakespeare has organized the incidents and events that he put into his text, is a very important part of trying to understand the process of how meanings are constructed by the text in performance. The order in which the audience sees the events unfolding is carefully contrived: certain events are scenically juxtaposed in order to give dramatic effect and meaning. Sometimes, the reason for the narrative sequence is immediately obvious, such as the opening three scenes of *A Midsummer Night's Dream* which serve the purpose of introducing the audience to the three contrasting worlds of the play: the court, the mechanicals and the fairies. In *Macbeth* too, the organizing principle at the opening of the play is quite clear, but, nonetheless, dramatically very effective. The action begins with a short scene depicting the witches on the heath; scene two is longer and slower in pace, showing the court of Duncan and introducing the audience to the name and reputation of Macbeth. The third scene brings Macbeth and the witches into confrontation, so setting up the spring ('the charm's wound up') that the subsequent action will uncoil.

Juxtaposing scenes and/or incidents can create dramatically contrasting moods. For example, the first scene of *Hamlet* generates a sense of general unease. It is ripe with tension brought about through an unresolved confrontation with supernatural forces. However, set against it in the scene that immediately follows (and in Shakespeare's theatre the convention was that scenes flowed into one another with the absolute minimum of interruption) is a very different spectacle. Here, uncertainty is displaced by a general sense of purpose; there is a clear focus on Claudius, seen exercising the diplomatic skills of a confident ruler going about the business of organizing his state.

One of the most memorable juxtapositions of incidents occurs, not in *Hamlet*, but in *Julius Caesar*. In Act Three, scene two, Mark Antony and Brutus both have an opportunity to address a crowd of plebeians following the assassination of their leader, Julius Caesar. Brutus, one of the leaders of the conspiracy to kill Caesar, and one who played an active role in his death, speaks to the angry and confused crowd in order to explain to them the reasons that led to such drastic, but, in the view of the conspirators, such necessary action. His on-stage audience starts from a position of hostility towards him, but his cool and rational speech succeeds in winning their attention and respect. Brutus uses a rhetorical trick to win their sympathy. He explains his action, and that of his fellow conspirators, as necessary because:

Not that I loved Caesar less, but that I loved Rome more. (III, ii, line 21)

Convincingly he is now speaking as their representative and his listeners respond positively:

FIRST PLEBEIAN This Caesar was a tyrant.

THIRD PLEBEIAN   Nay, that's certain.
  We are blest that Rome is rid of him.   (lines 70–1)

Brutus is speaking to two audiences, one on-stage and the other in the auditorium of the theatre. In this scene, as in all the others you read, you must use your imagination to stage the performance text, for without it the full impact of the scene will never be realized. The stage directions say that Brutus enters a pulpit; whatever this may have been on the Elizabethan stage, it is pretty clear that Shakespeare intended the actor to take up a commanding and, probably, elevated position for the speech. For the sake of argument, and because it is *necessary* to make a conscious decision about it, let us suppose that Brutus takes up a position up-stage of the plebeians so that when he addresses them, the focus on what he says, and the way in which he says it, includes the off-stage audience as well as that of the plebeians. Both, not only listen, but also respond. The actors, of course, have already calculated their response, but the audience has not; it is open to manipulation as a result of the experience of witnessing the discourse between one man and a large crowd. When Brutus has finished speaking it is the turn of Mark Antony. Let us assume that he too adopts an identical position on-stage (of course, you could provide a reason for him *not* doing so: he could deliberately refuse to elevate himself above the ordinary people and instead walk amongst them whilst delivering his oration). In his speech, Shakespeare has given the actor a terrific opportunity for a display of rhetorical fireworks. In all likelihood, audiences on- and off-stage are moved by the sheer force of Antony's rhetoric rather than by his argument. He works on the emotions of his listeners, associating himself constantly with his audience so that they are drawn to him. Most people, even those who don't know the play, will recognize his, 'Friends, Romans, countrymen, lend me your ears' (line 74), but few can really remember the substance of the argument that follows. But, almost as soon as Antony has claimed the plebeians as 'friends' (a tremendous irony in view of the way in which such people are treated throughout the play), their previous acceptance of Brutus's argument begins to be rapidly eclipsed. What, in the excitement and immediacy of performance has seemed an entirely reasonable position, is now transformed into an act of gross treachery, and the peaceful, passive, on-stage listeners become a violent avenging mob:

SECOND PLEBEIAN   Most noble Caesar! We'll revenge his death.
THIRD PLEBEIAN   O royal Caesar!   (lines 244–5)

The actor in the role of Mark Antony must set out to persuade and move *both* sets of audience; if he succeeds, the juxtaposing of this scene with the one that follows will make sure that the audience in the theatre *feels* the effects, and *sees* the results of what can happen when people are ruled by emotion and not by reason. There is an obvious but chilling parallel to be drawn by twentieth-century audiences still capable of recalling the devastating rhetoric of Adolf Hitler's Nuremberg rallies, who are alive to the reality of the deeds of carnage and waste to which those words ultimately led. Watching the end of this scene from *Julius Caesar*, when the enraged mob rush off stage looking for blood, the audience is still, however well it knows the play, hit in the solar plexus by Antony's staggering confirmation that he is fully aware of what he has done, and the forces his rhetoric has unleashed:

> Now let it work. Mischief, thou art afoot,
> Take thou what course thou wilt.
>
> (lines 262–3)

The true course of that mischief is now revealed. Antony has stirred up violent and irrational emotions that the audience will now see turned into violent acts. In scene three, Antony's exit is immediately followed by the entrance of the poet Cinna. He is confronted by the angry mob who, on discovering that his name happens to be shared with one of the conspirators, attack him in a most violent and obscene manner. The Third Plebeian, who, after listening to Brutus in the previous scene, has *agreed* that Caesar was a tyrant, and that, 'We are blest that Rome is rid of him', is now crying out at the top of his voice, 'Tear him, tear him!' The audience witnessing this in the theatre are compelled, unless they shut their eyes and put their fingers in their ears, to witness the full consequences of Antony's manipulative rhetoric – words *can* kill. The full impact of juxtaposing the action in this way is made all the more powerful if, as I suspect, Shakespeare's actors intended when they first staged it, many of the audience have allowed themselves to be moved and persuaded by the personality of Mark Antony. This charismatic figure has charmed them into feeling like accessories to murder, which, the play suggests, they may well be.

Punctuation

As we all know, punctuation can radically affect the meaning of words on the page. How and why Shakespeare's words are punctuated, either by editors or by performers, deserves some attention. As an example of the power of editorial punctuation I want to cite a non-Shakespearean source. There is a verse from a well-known nineteenth-century hymn that is currently omitted from contemporary hymn books. It occurs in Mrs C. F. Alexander's (1818–95) *All Things Bright and Beautiful*:

> The rich man in his castle,
> The poor man at his gate,
> God made them high or lowly,
> And ordered their estate.

As it was printed, it seemed as if the writer was claiming that God was responsible for social inequalities, and this was unacceptable to the more liberal contemporary theologians and the offending verse was omitted. But, there is a considerable degree of argument that what was printed was *not* what Mrs Alexander meant, and that the verse could, and should, be included in the hymn, provided it was punctuated as the author intended:

> The rich man in his castle,
> The poor man at his gate,
> God made them, high or lowly,
> And ordered their estate.

The comma in the third line after 'them' makes a tremendous difference to the way in which the verse is understood.

So much for editors. Actors also punctuate as they speak the text, and in doing so they can create radically different and sometimes contentious readings. For example, in Terry Hands's 1980 production of *As You Like It* for the RSC, in the Rosalind/Orlando wooing scene, Rosalind (disguised as Ganymede) asked the young and lovesick Orlando 'how long you would have her after you have possessed her?' Susan Fleetwood (Rosalind) stressed the first 'have' and inserted a brief pause after the second, thus giving an emphasis to 'possessed', and indicating that Rosalind was speculating on the inevitable sexual conclusion to this ritual courtship.

I began this book by asserting that the printed text of a play is incomplete and partial without the imagined or real dimension of performance. As we have seen, the printed text of Shakespeare's plays is continually being constructed by editors, directors and, not least, by performers. Indeed, every generation of readers and audiences re-experiences Shakespeare as part of a living, and, therefore, changing culture. If it were possible to exactly reproduce a production of *Hamlet* in the style of the 1890s, an audience of the 1990s would probably laugh it off the stage. This is not to suggest that our theatre, or our reading of

Shakespeare is superior to theirs, simply that we operate a different set of conventions and approach texts in different ways, looking at different questions and finding alternative solutions to those sought even a generation ago, let alone one hundred years ago. We remake Shakespeare in our own image to reflect our own concerns and preoccupations. That his texts are capable of carrying such a weight without appearing to feel the burden, is one of the principal reasons why he continues to dominate current theatre practice, and why the process of making and remaking text-into-performance is a worthwhile activity. In the next chapter I want to focus on how directors, designers and actors work together in order to construct a Shakespeare play in performance.

The Performer's Text

Because it raises interesting and contentious issues about the process of making text-into-performance, I want, in the first part of this chapter, to concentrate on how to read a Shakespeare play as if preparing to direct it in the theatre. The director, as the individual ultimately responsible for *all* artistic and interpretative matters concerning the process of taking a play from page to stage, is a relatively modern phenomenon. The first directors appeared in Britain in the mid nineteenth century, partly in response to the need for someone to coordinate the increasingly elaborate spectacle on the stage, with the performances of the actors. So far as we know, Shakespeare's theatre had no one occupying such a role. The theatrical conditions of his day (absolutely minimal time for rehearsal, and a vast repertory of plays) did not permit the luxury of supporting someone who did not contribute to the work of the company either as a writer or performer. A leading player and shareholder in the company such as Richard Burbage, or even Shakespeare himself, may have given minimal practical instruction to his fellow players in matters where it was required, for example, in order to prevent confusion on the playing area. Such advice might include the timing of exits and entrances, the grouping of actors at particular moments, stage business and any stunts that needed practice if they were to be carried off convincingly. Almost all the plays would have required some amount of rehearsal, and the more spectacular texts such as *The Tempest*, where the action requires not only an elaborate masque, but also a banquet to be 'discovered' and then to vanish, must have required a good deal of time to rehearse adequately. But all this is *staging*, not directing in the modern understanding of the word. In Shakespeare's theatre there was, as far as we know, no *interpretative* mediation by any one individual between what Shakespeare (or any other dramatist) had written, and what his company of players performed.

The Director

In today's theatre things are very different. Now, the director wields enormous power, not only over individuals (especially actors), but also over the whole way in which a performance text will be constructed.

27

Almost without exception, successful directors of Shakespeare in Britain are the products of a university education, usually, though not exclusively, one obtained at Oxford or Cambridge. Certainly since the young Peter Hall took over the running of the RSC in the 1960s, most of the directors employed there, such as Peter Brook, Trevor Nunn, and more recently, Nicholas Hytner, have been university graduates; the directorate appointed in 1990 to run the company, Adrian Noble and Michael Attenborough, are both graduates – of Bristol and Sussex universities respectively. All of them are likely to have studied Shakespeare, and will certainly be very aware of his status in British culture. Apart from what this reveals about the predominantly middle-class make up of British theatre, it also often means in practice that the rehearsal room resembles the seminar room, in which Shakespeare's text, and sometimes his life as well, are explored critically and analytically, with the director doubling in the role of teacher/lecturer. This is certainly what can happen when John Caird (who works frequently for the RSC) is directing, and I have no reason to think that his approach is exceptional:

I ask each actor to choose and research a subject which is in some way connected with the character he or she is playing. The actors then have to address their assembled colleagues on their chosen topic for ten minutes or so. In this way the whole company becomes expert about the period, and each individual actor becomes expert about the social, political and philosophical background from which their character was originally drawn ... Having chosen the subjects, a collegiate atmosphere begins to develop amongst the actors. They begin to swap research and books.   (Judith Cook, *Director's Theatre*, pp. 44–5)

When it comes to directing Shakespeare, most directors will have been employed because a particular theatre management believes that they will reinterpret a text, make the known and familiar seem fresh and new, and make audiences look again with new insights. Of course, there are some who feel that the pressure to come up with a 'new' interpretation of an old play creates a theatre designed to appeal to the intellectual vanity of the audience, by providing them with cleverly animated lectures on Shakespeare rather than emotionally gripping performances of his plays. Whether or not you agree, it is certainly true of theatre in general, and performances of Shakespeare in particular, that contemporary performance is director dominated, and designed to appeal as much to the intellect as the emotions.

Whilst it may be true that 'one of the central reasons why Shakespeare continues to be performed is not that there *is* a central realizable intention in each play that we still continue to value, but because we are still looking for the possibility of unforeseen meanings' (Jonathan Miller, *Subsequent Performances*, p. 64), such an approach emphasizes the modern director's task to *interpret* the text. But, the pressure on a director to arrive at what looks like a new reading of a Shakespeare play, or at least the pressure to avoid obvious references to past productions, is not the only difficulty that faces him or her. Finance, or the lack of it, is as important and influential now as it was when Shakespeare's plays first saw the light of day. Sometimes reputations, as well as a great deal of money, hang on the success or failure of the director's interpretation. The extent to which money is available in the first place can circumscribe the most fertile imagination, and limit what is desirable to what is affordable. Financial considerations will limit the amount of time available for rehearsal; the design of the production will have to fit in with the budget and casting will also be affected. Financial pressures also mean that directors will have to take creative decisions very early on in the pre-production stage, on which there will be no going back. Such decisions, particularly in the areas of casting and design, will inevitably not only open up a text in certain directions, but also close down others. Moreover, whatever interpretative line is taken by a director, the chosen playing space will also affect the way in which he or she thinks. If a play is to be performed in a small space – like the Pit or the Almeida theatre in London, or the Swan theatre at Stratford – the nature of the performance designed to fit it may differ considerably from one that will eventually occupy the open spaces at the Barbican theatre or the main house at Stratford-upon-Avon.

In spite of these restrictions, the modern theatre director is an individual who exercises considerable power and influence over the theatrical product eventually consumed by audiences. Potentially, his or her power is greater than that of any other person involved in the creative process of staging a play, including actors and dramatists. It is not only a minority of critics and academics who express concern at this situation, actors, in particular, often feel justifiably aggrieved when confronted with directors who implicitly reject the collective nature of theatrical work by paying lip service to democracy, whilst insisting ultimately on seeing a play in *their* way. However, for better or worse, it is now an established convention that performances of Shakespeare are often seen and appreciated only in terms of how their director constructed them. Thus, in the 1970s, people spoke of Shakespeare's *A Midsummer Night's Dream* as performed in 1970 by the RSC under the director Peter Brook, as 'Brook's Dream', and in the 1980s, younger directors have made their reputation through directing innovative

29

performances of Shakespeare such as Deborah Warner's Kick Theatre production of *King Lear*, and Nicholas Hytner's productions of *Measure for Measure*, *King Lear* and *The Tempest*, all for the RSC. The names of theatre directors are now as well known, and sometimes better known, than those of the actors they direct, and audiences may well be attracted to a new production of Shakespeare not because it is Shakespeare, but because a 'star' director is directing it. What all this means is that we cannot begin to understand the contemporary performer's text of Shakespeare unless we have first negotiated that of the director, in whose mind the original presentational strategies are charted.

However, the active reader is in an ideal production situation (that is, it is imaginary, and subject only to imaginative rather than budgetary constraints), you are free from the shackles of arts under-funding. Nonetheless, we need to make the imaginative process of *Shakespeare: Text into Performance* parallel the actual one as far as possible. To succeed in doing that we should first consider how a play is cast.

Casting

When Shakespeare is produced at the RSC or the National Theatre, the practice is usually to leave the decisions regarding the casting of the major roles entirely up to the play's director. Indeed, he or she may only have agreed to direct a particular play on the understanding that a specific actor is available to play a specific role. For instance, Hytner's decision to direct *The Tempest* for the RSC in 1989 was dependent upon John Wood's agreement to play Prospero, and the availability of that same actor ensured that Hytner would direct *King Lear*, with Wood as Lear, in 1990. Sometimes, the reasons for casting particular actors in certain roles remain unclear. However, often the reasons are obvious. For example, in Jonathan Miller's production of *King Lear* for the BBC/Time Life Shakespeare series (a production referred to in some detail later in this book), his casting of Michael Hordern as Lear contributed to an interpretation of the play which stressed its domestic, as opposed to, its universalist claims.

Just as casting particular actors and actresses, and the implications of the process, is a task that cannot be avoided in the theatre, casting should not be avoided by the active reader of plays. But, casting is a minefield through which to tread with extreme care, using intuition as well as reason for a guide. It is a process in which subjective judgements and prejudices are rife. Thinking, for a moment, about how we assess people when we meet them for the first time, may help us to see more clearly some of the problems and challenges presented to a director when casting a play. When we meet strangers we try to 'read' them. They generate a whole series of visual and aural signs which we interpret and filter through our own particular set of personal prejudices. We observe their choice of clothes, and how they are worn, their hairstyle and general physical characteristics; are they thin, fat, tall and so on? We listen to their speech; to accent, to the tone and pitch of the voice. From these, and from many more impressions, we construct a highly personal but influential first impression of what they are like. Do we find them attractive or unattractive, warm or cool, etc? Our first impressions will also include an assessment of their social selves, for example, their class, possibly their trade/profession, as well as providing clues to help in guessing at further aspects of their personality. Such impressions are, of course, coloured and formed by our own social attitudes – attitudes influenced by class, race and gender. When reading a Shakespeare play the immediate impulse is, literally, to see in the mind's eye a stereotype image of a character – Ophelia as a young, often blonde-haired, physically slight but attractive woman; Hamlet as physically attractive, athletic, youthful, tall and blond – without really considering *where* the image has come from, and its appropriateness or otherwise to our reading of the text. Often the image derives from previous productions of the play on stage or on film. Despite some exceptions, it remains generally true that, in Shakespeare reproduced, there is a powerful cliché which casts supposedly positive female characters, especially those associated with youth and innocence (like Ophelia or Perdita), with blonde-haired actresses, whilst more devious women (like Lady Macbeth or Cleopatra) will almost inevitably be played by dark-haired actresses.

Things are made somewhat easier if Shakespeare's text indicates clearly and unambiguously that a character possesses specific physical characteristics. These must be respected so long as a director is concerned with *interpretation*, as opposed to *adaptation*. For example, in *A Midsummer Night's Dream*, the actress chosen to play Helena should be taller than the one to play Hermia: the former is referred to as a 'painted maypole' (III, ii, line 296), and the latter as 'low' and 'little' (III, ii, line 326). In such a straightforward case, at least one issue of casting has already been dictated by the text. However, rarely is Shakespeare so helpfully explicit. Take the case of *Richard III*, for example: in that play, Richard, Duke of Gloucester, is variously described as 'deformed', 'unfinished', 'crookback', etc. This is a condition that

Shakespeare did not invent, but took from his main sources for the play, Sir Thomas More's *The History of King Richard the Third*, and Ralph Holinshed's *Chronicles of England, Scotland and Ireland*. An Elizabethan audience would almost certainly have interpreted the mis-shapen body of Richard as an outward manifestation of an inwardly deformed and twisted soul. We do not know what decisions the actor first charged with playing the role took in order to illustrate Richard's physical deformity. Nor do we know what that individual actually looked like. However, if we read *Richard III* today we inevitably have a very specific and graphic image of Richard in our heads. That image is almost certainly derived from performances of the role that we have witnessed or heard about from others. Arguably, the most notable in recent years have been those of Laurence Olivier and Antony Sher. Olivier made a film of his stage production which was released in 1953 and which, despite its age, continues to be widely shown (it is available on video). In his book *Year of the King*, recording his own preparations for playing Richard, Antony Sher acknowledged the extraordinary influence of Olivier's performance:

[it is] so famous that all round the world people can get up and do impersonations of it. At parties in New York, in bars in Naples, or remote Australian farms and forgotten South Sea Islands, people get to their feet, hoist one shoulder up, shrivel an arm and limp across the room declaring, 'Now is the winter,' or its linguistic equivalent. (p. 67)

Sher created his interpretation for an RSC production in 1983, directed by Bill Alexander, and, like Olivier, Sher's performance was celebrated not just in Britain, but also in the United States and Australia where the production toured. In performance, both actors, despite being separated by thirty years, chose to emphasize the *physical*, as opposed to the *moral* deformity of Richard. Antony Sher propelled himself about the stage on titanium crutches, and wore a grotesque artificial hump. But, despite the physical handicap he never let go of an approach to the role that, also, equally emphasized Richard's charismatic presence, charm and sexual potency. Both Sher and Olivier were well-known actors when cast in the role, and both used the performance not only as an opportunity to construct an *attractive* character, but also to display their own psycho/sexual potency as performers. The problem for most contemporary readers of *Richard III* is the difficulty they inevitably experience in attempting to divorce such powerful casting from their minds in order to think afresh about the role and its relationship to the play as a whole.

The memory of a particularly vivid interpretation of a role isn't always a handicap, and certainly has no need to become one provided the reader is aware of it. Sometimes, of course, the memory of a particular performance can be liberating and encouraging, as Frances Barber revealed when discussing her preparations for playing Ophelia in Ron Daniel's 1984 production of *Hamlet* for the RSC.

Harriet Walter – an actress I greatly admire – had played Ophelia [in Richard Eyre's production for the Royal Court Theatre] which dispelled any traditional images of the weak, stupid girl which may have been lurking in the minds of the audience. I carried this memory with me for many weeks preparing for the same role. (*Players of Shakespeare, Vol. II*, p. 137)

However, despite being influenced by Harriet Walter's work on Ophelia, Frances Barber certainly didn't imitate her when it came to constructing her own interpretation of the role. However, the active reader who succeeds in getting rid of one traditional image must also guard against the danger of replacing it with another. It is *not* an easy task to break the mould past performances have established in the minds of performers and readers. But, however inspired the original casting may have been, there is no such thing as a *definitive* performance. Active readers, like good actors, *have* to go on asking their own questions of *Shakespeare*'s text, and in doing so, arrive at their own interpretation rather than relying entirely on second-hand answers from someone else – critics or performers – however much they may be admired.

Thus, when casting a play in the imagination, the reader must carefully examine the appropriateness of the immediate images of individual characters that spring to mind, whether or not they are derived from known sources. We have to slow down the imaginative reproduction of the action and be willing to explore, and if necessary challenge, what often turn out to be crude stereotypes. Why should Richard III be a sexy charismatic figure; isn't he also a moral ogre?

Casting doesn't always involve purely subjective judgements. The age of a particular performer can be an obvious factor and influence the interpretation of the character he or she is playing, as well as the play as a whole. In Jonathan Miller's production of *King Lear* at the Old Vic in London in 1989, he cast the roles of Goneril and Regan with two middle-aged actresses (Gemma Jones and Frances de la Tour, respectively) in order to emphasize the difficulties these women – and many *contemporary* women – face in having to accommodate a difficult elderly parent (Lear) within their households. In the same production

Miller also gave a good illustration of how casting can open up one reading of the text whilst closing others. Edmund was played by Clive Russell, an actor of great physical presence; he was tall, muscular and bearded. From the moment he was first seen in Act One, scene one, lolling against a wall of the set, his physical presence made Edmund seem almost a different species from the rest of the characters, a difference clearly signalled not only by his looks, but also by his laid-back posture of casual self-assurance. He was, to twentieth-century eyes, a Laurentian figure whose affinity with the natural world ('Nature thou art my goddess') gave him a power that helped to explain his almost mesmeric fatal attraction for both Goneril and Regan.

In his 1973 production of *The Tempest* for the National Theatre, Peter Hall cast the actor Michael Feast as Ariel. The text that Hall was constructing required an Ariel who was 'sexless', and Michael Feast was chosen because of what Hall saw as his androgynous quality. In the same production, Hall made a similar (critical) decision regarding the casting of Ferdinand and Miranda: that they 'should of course be very young'. But, there is no 'of course'. Hall's decision as to how to cast all three roles is both legitimate and necessary, but it is a subjective, evaluative statement about *his* text at a particular but crucial moment in its genesis. In a production of the same play at the Old Vic in 1988, Jonathan Miller cast Ariel with a black actor, Cyril Nri. Caliban was also played by a black actor, Rudolph Walker. Presumably, Miller's casting was done in this way in order to make a point about who is, and who is not, native to the island, and to suggest a link between white colonialism and black exploitation. Prospero was thus associated with colonialism as he took over the island and subjected its native inhabitants to his will.

Terry Hands, until recently the director of the Royal Shakespeare Company, considers the casting of a play one of the most important but difficult tasks that fall to any director. He provided a fine example of theatrically effective and textually significant casting in his 1980 production of *Richard II* for the RSC. His choice of Alan Howard as Richard, and David Suchet as Bolingbroke/Henry IV, made not only possible but also theatrically credible a text which, in performance, articulated two very different and conflicting statements about kingship and the exercise of political power. Often it is necessary to treat these opposing elements in *Richard II* as mutually exclusive, so Hands's inspired casting provided a subtle and effective dimension to his director's text. Alan Howard is a tall, physically lithe and elegant actor, with blond hair, blue eyes and a fine ringing tenor voice: in short, an actor, by nature capable of projecting an image of a heroic male stereotype. The physical dimension of the character seemed to resemble a medieval icon, of whom it was easy for an audience to accept unquestioningly that he was 'not born to sue, but to command' (I, i, line 196). Especially in the first half of the play, before the deposition scene, Alan Howard's performer's text showed a king in love with his own public image; an image built upon complete familiarity and ease with the exploitation of public ceremony and ritual. This Richard was a born actor, and enacted the role of the king with a considerable measure of skill and sheer joy in its execution. Watching him in the play's ceremonial scenes, the audience experienced no difficulty in recognizing the truth of York's statement on the occasion of Richard's return from Ireland to confront the revolt led by Bolingbroke.

> Yet looks he like a king. Behold his eye.
> As bright as is the eagle's, lightens forth
> Controlling majesty. Alack, alack for woe
> That any harm should stain so fair a show!
> (III, iii, lines 68–71)

The subsequent traumatic events of Richard's deposition were genuinely *felt* by the audience because of the loss they had experienced from watching a 'well graced actor' and master showman controlling a spectacle.

David Suchet's Bolingbroke, on the other hand, was presented both through his physical appearance and the actor's reading of the role as a very different kind of individual to the Richard of Alan Howard. Suchet is short, dark and stockily built. He lacks the elegance and flamboyance of Alan Howard. In casting him in the role of Henry IV, Terry Hands was able to illustrate a man who ruled through a grasp of the political rather than the ceremonial world. David Suchet's King resembled the modern political ruler rather than the idealized medieval monarch which seemed to be embodied in Alan Howard's Richard. Suchet's Henry IV was graphically shown to be a man more at home behind a desk than on a throne. Indeed, in Terry Hands's production, the new king discarded the brilliant costumes preferred by his predecessor – and which looked so fine on him – in favour of muted colours and a large crucifix. So unused (and uneasy) to wearing a crown was he that, in the scene showing him in his new role following Richard's eclipse, he chose to keep it on a desk in front of him rather than on his head.

When making his 1955 film version of *Richard III*, Olivier (who directed the film and also cast himself as Richard) made equally significant decisions. At the time of making the film, Olivier was a very popular actor, both on the stage and in the cinema, and had been knighted by the young Queen Elizabeth II for services to the theatre. Olivier's popularity as an actor was built on his romantic/heroic screen roles, such as Heathcliffe in William Wyler's 1939 film of *Wuthering Heights*, and Henry V, who he played in the film that he directed in 1944 to coincide with the Normandy landings and the last days of the Second World War. His second Shakespeare film, *Hamlet* (1948), was a highly romanticized version of the play in which, at the age of forty-one, Olivier cast himself in the role of the Prince. In his career prior to *Richard III*, Olivier had largely avoided playing unattractive or unsympathetic characters, and he was determined from the start that his Richard III should be no exception. In casting other roles, Olivier took decisions that radically affected the range of interpretation open to a cinema audience, many of whom, he assumed, would be coming to the film with no prior knowledge of the play either as a literary text or as a theatrical performance. In casting one of the few women's roles his choice of Claire Bloom as Lady Anne proved crucial. Another crucial decision was to omit the character of Queen Margaret; in doing so, he effectively denied his audience the opportunity of witnessing the one character in the play who is a theatrical match (at least for a time) for Richard. Margaret is not only a potentially powerful theatrical force, she also presents a distinctly unpleasant and accurate picture of Richard as the 'bottled spider'. However, it is Olivier's casting of Lady Anne that I want to examine in detail.

One of the most celebrated scenes in the play, and one of the most memorable in the film, Act One, scene two, is the so-called 'wooing' scene. In Shakespeare's text, Richard confronts Lady Anne as she is conducting the funeral arrangements for her father-in-law, Henry VI, whom Richard has killed; Richard has also been responsible for killing Anne's husband. At the beginning of the scene she is fully aware of what he has done, but, despite these apparently insurmountable odds, by the end of the scene (usually less than fifteen minutes' playing time), Richard seems to have succeeded in winning a promise from her, not only of forgiveness, but also of future admission to her bedchamber. If the scene is unfamiliar to you please take this opportunity of reading it.

Enter the corse of Henry the Sixth, with halberds to guard it; Lady Anne being the mourner, attended by Tressel and Berkeley

ANNE

　Set down, set down your honourable load –
　If honour may be shrouded in a hearse –

Whilst I awhile obsequiously lament
Th'untimely fall of virtuous Lancaster.
    The bearers set down the hearse
Poor key-cold figure of a holy king,
Pale ashes of the house of Lancaster,
Thou bloodless remnant of that royal blood,
Be it lawful that I invocate thy ghost
To hear the lamentations of poor Anne,
Wife to thy Edward, to thy slaughtered son   10
Stabbed by the selfsame hand that made these wounds!
Lo, in these windows that let forth thy life
I pour the helpless balm of my poor eyes.
O, cursèd be the hand that made these holes!
Cursèd the heart that had the heart to do it!
Cursèd the blood that let this blood from hence!
More direful hap betide that hated wretch
That makes us wretched by the death of thee
Than I can wish to wolves – to spiders, toads,
Or any creeping venomed thing that lives!   20
If ever he have child, abortive be it,
Prodigious, and untimely brought to light,
Whose ugly and unnatural aspect
May fright the hopeful mother at the view,
And that be heir to his unhappiness!
If ever he have wife, let her be made
More miserable by the life of him
Than I am made by my young lord and thee!
Come now, towards Chertsey with your holy load,
Taken from Paul's to be interrèd there.   30
    The bearers take up the hearse
And still, as you are weary of this weight,
Rest you, whiles I lament King Henry's corse.
    Enter Richard, Duke of Gloucester

RICHARD
  Stay, you that bear the corse, and set it down.
ANNE
  What black magician conjures up this fiend
  To stop devoted charitable deeds?
RICHARD
  Villains, set down the corse, or, by Saint Paul,
  I'll make a corse of him that disobeys!
GENTLEMAN
  My lord, stand back, and let the coffin pass.
RICHARD
  Unmannered dog! Stand thou, when I command!

Advance thy halberd higher than my breast,   40
Or, by Saint Paul, I'll strike thee to my foot
And spurn upon thee, beggar, for thy boldness.

The bearers set down the hearse

ANNE

What, do you tremble? Are you all afraid?
Alas, I blame you not, for you are mortal,
And mortal eyes cannot endure the devil.
Avaunt, thou dreadful minister of hell!
Thou hadst but power over his mortal body;
His soul thou canst not have. Therefore, be gone.

RICHARD

Sweet saint, for charity, be not so curst.

ANNE

Foul devil, for God's sake hence, and trouble us not,   50
For thou hast made the happy earth thy hell,
Filled it with cursing cries and deep exclaims.
If thou delight to view thy heinous deeds,
Behold this pattern of thy butcheries.
O gentlemen, see, see! Dead Henry's wounds
Open their congealed mouths and bleed afresh!
Blush, blush, thou lump of foul deformity;
For 'tis thy presence that exhales this blood
From cold and empty veins where no blood dwells.
Thy deed inhuman and unnatural   60
Provokes this deluge most unnatural.
O God, which this blood mad'st, revenge his death!
O earth, which this blood drink'st, revenge his death!
Either heaven with lightning strike the murderer dead;
Or earth gape open wide and eat him quick,
As thou dost swallow up this good King's blood
Which his hell-governed arm hath butchered!

RICHARD

Lady, you know no rules of charity,
Which renders good for bad, blessings for curses.

ANNE

Villain, thou know'st nor law of God nor man: 70
No beast so fierce but knows some touch of pity.

RICHARD

But I know none, and therefore am no beast.

ANNE

O wonderful, when devils tell the truth!

RICHARD

More wonderful, when angels are so angry.
Vouchsafe, divine perfection of a woman,

Of these supposèd crimes to give me leave
By circumstance but to acquit myself.

ANNE
Vouchsafe, diffused infection of a man
Of these known evils, but to give me leave
By circumstance to accuse thy cursèd self.   80

RICHARD
Fairer than tongue can name thee, let me have
Some patient leisure to excuse myself.

ANNE
Fouler than heart can think thee, thou canst make
No excuse current but to hang thyself.

RICHARD
By such despair I should accuse myself.

ANNE
And by despairing shalt thou stand excused
For doing worthy vengeance on thyself
That didst unworthy slaughter upon others.

RICHARD
Say that I slew them not.

ANNE   Then say they were not slain.
But dead they are, and, devilish slave, by thee.   90

RICHARD
I did not kill your husband.

ANNE   Why, then he is alive.

RICHARD
Nay, he is dead, and slain by Edward's hands.

ANNE
In thy foul throat thou li'st! Queen Margaret saw
Thy murderous falchion smoking in his blood;
The which thou once didst bend against her breast,
But that thy brothers beat aside the point.

RICHARD
I was provokèd by her slanderous tongue
That laid their guilt upon my guiltless shoulders.

ANNE
Thou wast provokèd by thy bloody mind
That never dream'st on aught but butcheries.   100
Didst thou not kill this King?

RICHARD   I grant ye – yea.

ANNE
Dost grant me, hedgehog? Then God grant me too
Thou mayst be damnèd for that wicked deed!
O, he was gentle, mild, and virtuous!

RICHARD

   The better for the King of Heaven that hath him.

ANNE

   He is in heaven, where thou shalt never come.

RICHARD

   Let him thank me that holp to send him thither;

   For he was fitter for that place than earth.

ANNE

   And thou unfit for any place, but hell.

RICHARD

   Yes, one place else, if you will hear me name it.   110

ANNE

   Some dungeon.

RICHARD   Your bedchamber.

ANNE

   Ill rest betide the chamber where thou liest!

RICHARD

   So will it, madam, till I lie with you.

ANNE

   I hope so.

RICHARD   I know so. But gentle Lady Anne,

   To leave this keen encounter of our wits

   And fall something into a slower method,

   Is not the causer of the timeless deaths

   Of these Plantagenets, Henry and Edward,

   As blameful as the executioner?

ANNE

   Thou wast the cause and most accursèd effect.   120

RICHARD

   Your beauty was the cause of that effect –

   Your beauty, that did haunt me in my sleep

   To undertake the death of all the world,

   So I might live one hour in your sweet bosom.

ANNE

   If I thought that, I tell thee, homicide,

   These nails should rent that beauty from my cheeks.

RICHARD

   These eyes could not endure that beauty's wrack;

   You should not blemish it, if I stood by.

   As all the world is cheerèd by the sun,

   So I by that. It is my day, my life.   130

ANNE

   Black night o'ershade thy day, and death thy life!

RICHARD

   Curse not thyself, fair creature – thou art both.

ANNE
> I would I were, to be revenged on thee.

RICHARD
> It is a quarrel most unnatural
> To be revenged on him that loveth thee.

ANNE
> It is a quarrel just and reasonable
> To be revenged on him that killed my husband.

RICHARD
> He that bereft thee, lady, of thy husband
> Did it to help thee to a better husband.

ANNE
> His better doth not breathe upon the earth.   140

RICHARD
> He lives, that loves thee better than he could.

ANNE
> Name him.

RICHARD   Plantagenet.

ANNE   Why that was he.

RICHARD
> The selfsame name, but one of better nature.

ANNE
> Where is he?

RICHARD   Here.
> *She spits at him*
>   Why dost thou spit at me?

ANNE
> Would it were mortal poison for thy sake!

RICHARD
> Never came poison from so sweet a place.

ANNE
> Never hung poison on a fouler toad.
> Out of my sight! Thou dost infect mine eyes.

RICHARD
> Thine eyes, sweet lady, have infected mine.

ANNE
> Would they were basilisks to strike thee dead!   150

RICHARD
> I would they were, that I might die at once,
> For now they kill me with a living death.
> Those eyes of thine from mine have drawn salt tears,
> Shamed their aspects with store of childish drops.
> These eyes, which never shed remorseful tear –
> No, when my father York and Edward wept
> To hear the piteous moan that Rutland made

When black-faced Clifford shook his sword at him;
Nor when thy warlike father, like a child,
Told the sad story of my father's death 160
And twenty times made pause to sob and weep,
That all the standers-by had wet their cheeks
Like trees bedashed with rain – in that sad time
My manly eyes did scorn an humble tear;
And what these sorrows could not thence exhale,
Thy beauty hath, and made them blind with weeping.
I never sued to friend nor enemy;
My tongue could never learn sweet smoothing word;
But, now thy beauty is proposed my fee,
My proud heart sues, and prompts my tongue to speak. 170
    She looks scornfully at him
Teach not thy lip such scorn; for it was made
For kissing, lady, not for such contempt.
If thy revengeful heart cannot forgive,
Lo, here I lend thee this sharp-pointed sword,
Which if thou please to hide in this true breast
And let the soul forth that adoreth thee,
I lay it naked to the deadly stroke
And humbly beg the death upon my knee.
    He lays his breast open. She offers at it with his sword
Nay, do not pause, for I did kill King Henry –
But 'twas thy beauty that provokèd me. 180
Nay now, dispatch, 'twas I that stabbed young Edward –
But 'twas thy heavenly face that set me on.
    She falls the sword
Take up the sword again, or take up me.

ANNE

Arise, dissembler; though I wish thy death
I will not be thy executioner.

RICHARD

Then bid me kill myself, and I will do it.

ANNE

I have already.

RICHARD   That was in thy rage.
Speak it again, and even with the word
This hand, which for thy love did kill thy love,
Shall for thy love kill a far truer love; 190
To both their deaths shalt thou be accessory.

ANNE

I would I knew thy heart.

42

RICHARD
  'Tis figured in my tongue.
ANNE
  I fear me both are false.
RICHARD
  Then never was man true.
ANNE
  Well, well put up your sword.
RICHARD
  Say then my peace is made.
ANNE
  That shalt thou know hereafter.
RICHARD
  But shall I live in hope?
ANNE
  All men, I hope, live so.   200
RICHARD
  Vouchsafe to wear this ring.
ANNE
  To take is not to give.
        She puts on the ring
RICHARD
  Look how my ring encompasseth thy finger,
  Even so thy breast encloseth my poor heart.
  Wear both of them, for both of them are thine;
  And if thy poor devoted servant may
  But beg one favour at thy gracious hand,
  Thou dost confirm his happiness for ever.
ANNE
  What is it?
RICHARD
  That it may please you leave these sad designs   210
  To him that hath more cause to be a mourner,
  And presently repair to Crosby House;
  Where, after I have solemnly interred
  At Chertsey monastery this noble king
  And wet his grave with my repentant tears,
  I will with all expedient duty see you.
  For divers unknown reasons, I beseech you,
  Grant me this boon.
ANNE
  With all my heart; and much it joys me too
  To see you are become so penitent.   220
  Tressel and Berkeley, go along with me.

RICHARD
  Bid me farewell.
ANNE   'Tis more than you deserve;
  But since you teach me how to flatter you,
  Imagine I have said farewell already.

> *Exeunt Tressel and Berkeley, with Anne*

RICHARD
  Sirs, take up the corse.
GENTLEMAN   Towards Chertsey, noble lord?
RICHARD
  No, to Whitefriars – there attend my coming.

> *Exeunt bearers and guard with corse*

Olivier believed that the scene, as Shakespeare wrote it, was asking far too much of cinema audiences by expecting them to believe in the credibility of the events it narrates. In fact, Olivier exacerbated the problem by changing the dramatist's text to make the corpse that of Anne's husband instead of that of her father-in-law! What Olivier obviously wanted to emphasize in *his* text, both as an actor and director, was Richard's ability as a lover: the prize was great, and the barriers to its possession enormous. To give the 'wooing' scene a chance of appearing convincing, Olivier decided to split the scene into two distinct halves by inserting an earlier episode, in which Clarence is led off to the Tower, at the point where Anne exhibited the first signs of a change in her attitude towards Richard. This effected a passing of time and when Anne is next seen in the film the funeral is over, she is no longer in mourning, and stands, not beside the body of her husband, but leaning against his concrete tomb. Thus, the second half of the 'wooing' scene is made a private, rather than a public event, that takes place at an unspecified time after the funeral. Olivier's Richard no longer has to compete for attention with a bleeding corpse, nor with the on-stage presence of Tressel and Berkeley and those who were carrying the body to burial. The break in the scene was intended to give psychological credibility to Richard and Anne's extraordinary actions:

On the stage the wooing of Lady Anne works brilliantly, but if it's too sudden on the screen the unaccustomed audience would cry, 'Hold. We don't believe this!' So I cut the scene in two, let time pass . . .   (*On Acting*, p. 206)

Thirty years later, Antony Sher shared the same misgivings about this famous episode:

Richard woos Lady Anne (his most unlikely conquest in the play; I've never seen it work) by being pathetic, vulnerable. She feels sorry for him, is convinced he couldn't hurt a fly.   (*Year of the King*, p. 18)

But, is what either actor says really true? Would a cinema audience (or *any* audience) really find difficulty in accepting the credibility of the wooing? Part, at least, of the answer lies not only in the way in which Richard is cast and played, but also in the casting of the role of Lady Anne: Olivier, as already mentioned, chose Claire Bloom.

Claire Bloom was not only generally considered conventionally beautiful, but also, she was an actress capable of displaying a strong sense of self-confidence and maturity. However, the more impressive the physical presence of the actress playing Anne, the greater difficulty the audience will have in accepting her seduction as believable and consistent with her character. The scene, as written by Shakespeare, shows events that take place in a context laden with grief and death: Lady Anne is escorting the body of a dead King to his grave. If you wish to approach the text psychologically (and Olivier certainly did) then you might recall that on such occasions as funerals those most closely involved with the deceased are extremely vulnerable. They may need, and they may seek, consolation wherever they can find it, for it is an occasion characterized by emotional turmoil and confusion. If, in the role of Anne, an actress is cast who looks young – perhaps very young, say fifteen or sixteen – and who is physically slight and not especially beautiful (we have only Richard's evidence to indicate her physical qualities, and he is hardly the most reliable source), immediately, the scope for display by Anne of *her* vulnerability will have been greatly enhanced.

When you, the reader, come to cast this role, you should also turn your attention to other characters who appear in this scene but who tend to receive very little critical attention. Despite this, Tressel, Berkeley and the pallbearers are important keys in unlocking a reading of the action neglected by Olivier. If all the male characters in the scene, excluding Richard, are played by tall and powerfully built actors, then the audience will see a spectacle in which a very young woman is isolated and vulnerable; she is the only woman present, and has no obvious allies. Yet she, the least physically impressive person on-stage, has the most difficult task to enact. It is *her* difficulty that this casting emphasizes; not Richard's difficulty in wooing her. Lady Anne must both bury a King, and publicly 'obsequiously lament/Th'untimely fall of virtuous Lancaster'. For Laurence Olivier's Richard to successfully seduce Claire Bloom's Anne in the time and space given by Shakespeare might, indeed, have failed to convince *any* audience. But, had Olivier's Richard been seen to seduce not a mature woman, but a near-child at a funeral, his soliloquy at the end of the scene, 'Was ever woman in this humour wooed?/Was ever woman in this humour won?', might have a hollow, rather than a victorious ring to it. For, what an audience could see in this version of the scene is a 'conflict' or a challenge in which the eventual 'victory' is negligible because the battle was always between grossly unequal forces. Thus, interpretation can be reinforced by thoughtful use of the large numbers of vocally silent, but dramatically expressive, minor characters required by the action. We will return to them, and to this interesting scene, at a later stage.

Cutting

Deliberately and consciously deciding to cast a play as you read it is almost always a profitable exercise. Although it can be a difficult task, the problems faced are nothing when compared to those you will encounter if, in your director's text you find it necessary, as Olivier did, to cut or adapt the text of Shakespeare. It is common practice in the professional theatre, particularly in the production of classic texts, for a director to change what a dramatist has written, or, at least, to change what has been printed of what a dramatist is *thought* to have written by the omission of some part of it, or even by the addition of some new material. We have moved a good way from the fashion of the late nineteenth century when the great exponent of classical acting, and the acting profession's first knight, Henry Irving, was accused by the dramatist and critic George Bernard Shaw of not simply cutting Shakespeare, but disembowelling him. But it is very rare indeed to find a contemporary production of a Shakespeare play that has not been cut to some extent. John Barton, in his work as a director for the RSC, sometimes aroused wrath and indignation by his habit of changing the order of the scenes, or adding to Shakespeare's text portions written by himself, and by taking selected extracts from other Shakespeare plays and incorporating them into different productions. Other directors working for the RSC regularly make cuts, but justify them as an attempt to clarify an issue or sharpen the focus of the audience:

We cut Friar Lawrence's long recapitulation [of the events leading to the tragic deaths of Romeo and Juliet] ... with the idea of not allowing the audience to find comfort in distancing themselves from the situation through a long passage

of narrative. (Niamh Cusack, on Michael Bogdanov's 1986 production of
Romeo and Juliet for the RSC in *Players of Shakespeare, Vol. II*, p. 129)

Of course, if a student of dramatic literature suddenly begins to rewrite
Shakespeare, or pretend a scene or speech isn't in the play, he or she may
get in deep trouble with examiners. There is, however, an equal danger
in an over-reverential attitude to Shakespeare's plays which can inhibit
the necessary creative thinking required to move from printed text into
performance text. Cutting or adapting a text raises the tricky problem
of fidelity to the original.

Theatrical Fidelity

In 1989 a great fuss was made in the tabloid press in Britain over
remarks made by the head of the English department of the grammar
school at Stratford-upon-Avon where Shakespeare may (or may not)
have been a pupil. He was quoted as apparently discouraging his pupils
from visiting the RSC to watch Shakespeare because he believed there
were too many 'gimmicky' productions. It is difficult to know exactly
what he had in mind, but, in all probability, he would have disapproved
of the radical cutting and rearrangement of the text as had occurred in
Michael Bogdanov's 1986 RSC production of *Romeo and Juliet*. Not
only were speeches cut (referred to above) and the prologue moved to
the end of the play, but the setting was updated to contemporary Italy.

The arguments concerning theatrical fidelity to Shakespeare are not
new; they certainly go back as far as the Elizabethan theatre. Shakespeare's plays, in particular, have always been the site of a struggle for
possession of what they are, and are not, made to mean. In contemporary society, scholars (and schoolmasters) contest the legitimacy
of various conflicting interpretations of the plays. The theatre is also a
site for struggle. There, the competing claims for the authority of different texts (for example, those constructed by directors, actors, designers
as well as by dramatists) inevitably raises the question: is there such a
thing as a legitimate interpretation of Shakespeare? Can we ever know,
and should we seek to find out, what he intended? How much freedom
should actors, directors, designers, and, not least, students of Shakespeare (or any dramatic literature) allow themselves in making an imaginary performance? I find it impossible to give a definitive answer.
Many of those whose job it is to interpret Shakespeare's plays on the
professional stage, among them, for instance, Jonathan Miller, argue
for absolute freedom to use a dramatist's text (including Shakespeare's)

in any way they see fit. They argue that the criteria for judging the legitimacy of the exercise should be the theatricality of the resulting product and nothing else. They also argue that purely literary criteria are inappropriate in a theatrical context. Thus, if an idea works in performance, if audiences appear to like it and respond to it, there is sufficient justification for using it. But there are some, including equally well-known directors, who find this approach an anathema. William Gaskill, a director long-associated with London's Royal Court theatre – a theatre particularly identified with the development of new writing – finds no trouble in seeing what Shakespeare intended and acting on it: 'Jonathan Miller thinks it is impossible to know a writer's intentions and that it is not the director's business to try. I think this is plainly untrue' (*A Sense of Direction*, p. 139). However, there are undoubtedly some, those who Peter Brook calls 'deadly spectators' (*The Empty Space*, p. 32), who want and expect to have their *personal* prejudices reinforced, rather than challenged, when watching Shakespeare in the theatre.

As far as the active reader of plays is concerned, he or she will know from the start that *any* performance is *an* interpretation, and that it is impossible to construct a neutral or 'timeless' reading any more than it is possible to reconstruct a 'definitive' interpretation, or, still less, to present with absolute certainty what Shakespeare intended. If a distinction needs to be made between interpreting and adapting Shakespeare (if only because of the dictates of some public examinations), then it should stop at the rewriting of the spoken text despite the fact that a considerable amount of evidence suggests that this was common Elizabethan playhouse practice. If, for example, on reading *King Lear* you decide to cast an actor in his late forties as the King because you are tired of productions that suggest that Lear's abdication was the action of a worn-out and near-senile old man, and wish, instead, to suggest that it was a positive decision of one in command of all his faculties who decided to opt for the pleasures of premature retirement, eventually you will come up against a line where Lear states his age.

> I am a very foolish fond old man,
> Four score and upward.
>   (IV, vii, lines 60–1)

How old is old is here answered clearly: over eighty. The only way around this fact is to omit the line or rewrite it. Even if we stop short of rewriting Shakespeare, an enormous range of creative interpretations remain open, some of which may arouse the anguished cries of those who see it as their task to defend *Shakespeare*'s right of self-expression.

Updating

Fierce arguments about fidelity to Shakespeare are provoked, not only by cutting the texts, but also by the decision to change the historical period in which the action is set. Some examples are found in Bill Alexander's production of *The Merry Wives of Windsor* for the RSC, which he set in Britain in the 1950s, or Howard Davies's production of *Troilus and Cressida*, for the same company, set during the Crimean War. Both directors articulately defend these radical changes on the grounds that they illuminated the text for a modern audience. For Bill Alexander,

There are great similarities between the late Elizabethan–early Jacobean age and the late 1950s. It seemed to me a perfect parallel, more than any other period you could pick on. Morals were free enough for people like Falstaff to think they could get away with it, while there was also the incomprehensibility of what the new upward social mobility meant to women of working-class origin – actually, they would be the last people on earth to be seduced by an old aristocrat and this was exactly what Shakespeare was writing about.

(*Director's Theatre*, p. 66)

Howard Davies's decision came about as a result of his conviction that 'the Crimean War was the last of the romantic wars and it was only when people began to read *The Times* reports that they woke up to the fact that it was a dreary mess, not a romantic episode' (*Director's Theatre*, p. 78). Another general reason for updating the setting is because of the archaic language of Elizabethan/Jacobean England. Although Shakespeare's language is beautiful to some, it represents a formidable barrier to many others. Creating a recognizable context for that language to be spoken in, arguably helps an audience find the experience of watching Shakespeare less strange and forbidding, and, in addition, helps them to connect certain ideas and issues in the play with contemporary, ideas and issues of relevance to them. Michael Bogdanov, an English director, always produces Shakespeare in an updated, often contemporary context. His 1986 RSC production of *Romeo and Juliet* set the play in Italy during the 1960s, a world of fast cars, motorbikes and the Mafia. More recently (1989), Bogdanov's own company, the English Shakespeare Company, have toured Britain and much of the rest of the world with plays from the history cycle, *Richard II* to *Richard III*. His declared aim is always to try to find *new* audiences for Shakespeare, and, without patronizing them, or without diminishing Shakespeare, use his actors to create a relevant and exciting contemporary theatrical spectacle:

Critical Studies: Shakespeare: Text into Performance

The kind of theatre I try to create through Shakespeare is one of accessibility, one that doesn't take anything for granted. You start from the premise that nobody's seen or read the plays before – Shakespeare frequently takes that standpoint because he often tells you the story over and over again. *Richard II* [in Bogdanov's production for his English Shakespeare Company] is roughly set in the Regency period, the two parts of *Henry IV* and *Henry V* in an era not unlike that of the 1914–18 War, coming through the *Henry VI* (the plays being cut and arranged in three parts) to a Fascist *Richard III*.

(*Director's Theatre*, p. 84)

Those who like Bogdanov's approach, applaud his decision to resist playing Shakespeare as if the plays were merely stories from the distant past, full of pageantry and poetry. They see his decision to update the setting, to draw a parallel between the military adventurism of Henry V with that of Margaret Thatcher's Falklands war, as justifiable and relevant, raising important issues about individual and collective responsibility, political leadership and nationalism.

The Falklands conflict united the country in exactly the same kind of jingoistic way Henry V chose to unite his people against France. There are great parallels to be made. (*Director's Theatre*, pp. 84–5)

Bogdanov is by no means the only director to set Shakespeare in a contemporary context in order to use the past to help make sense of the present. Jonathan Miller's production of *The Merchant of Venice* for the National Theatre (available on video), with Laurence Olivier as Shylock, was set in Venice in the late nineteenth century, and made Miller's theatrical reputation. Miller was applauded, not only for drawing a fine performance out of Olivier, but also because his decision to bring the action forward to the late nineteenth century enabled audiences to associate the action, not with the Venice known and loved by tourists as an architectural nirvana, but with a real and thoroughly *commercial* city devoted to the values of competitive business and commerce. However, the transposition of the action didn't please everyone and affords a good example of the clash between a director's and an actor's text. Ian McDiarmid played Shylock in John Caird's production of the play for the RSC in 1984:

I made one stipulation when I accepted the part: the production should be set in Renaissance Venice rather than in a period and location which might emphasize some of the play's themes at the expense of others. 'Period' or modern dress productions of Shakespeare, while often successful in creating a strong social framework for the plays, can often distort the text and diminish the possibilities of choice for the actor, being an impediment rather than a stimulant to the imagination. There was much to admire in Jonathan Miller's television version of his National Theatre production of the play. A café setting seemed quite appropriate for the opening scene but when I felt I recognized it as Florian's on St Mark's Square, it seemed as anachronistic as American Express and also at odds with the world of the play. The setting also seemed to demand a naturalism which the verse could not sustain. An attempt to pin down an idea resulted in oversimplification.   (*Players of Shakespeare, Vol. II*, p. 50)

There are times when contemporary dramatists become extremely agitated about how 'their' play is produced on stage, and, of course, as Shakespeare cannot speak for himself there are bound to be those eager to speak for him, and to protect him from the attentions of 'trendy' directors and selfish actors. There are also those, such as Peter Hall, who feel that the spoken language of Elizabethan England will always be at odds with any modern setting. But, the whole issue as to what is and is not legitimate essentially comes down to a matter of individual judgement, of balancing the demands made by the printed text with those of the performers. Above all, theatre works most effectively when it is at its most collaborative and cooperative. Texts written by dramatists have to be translated by others into performances, and part of that legitimate process of transition may, surely, occasionally mean changing the location indicated by Shakespeare.

The tension that is sometimes manifested between the conflicting interests of dramatists and directors is not a recent phenomenon, only the form in which it manifests itself is new. In the nineteenth century, the argument was between the rights of the dramatist and those of the actor, and the actor-manager in particular. Although Shakespeare was seldom updated in the way illustrated above, he was subjected to *extensive* cutting. Sir Henry Irving cut *The Merchant of Venice* after the humiliated Shylock's final departure at the end of the trial scene (IV, i). Irving himself was playing Shylock, and, of course, there is no call on him in the final act of the drama. The practice of radically editing Shakespeare persisted throughout the nineteenth century, as, indeed, it had done in the seventeenth and eighteenth, where the plays were often not simply cut, but rewritten by Nahum Tate and others: 'the first rude sketches Shakespeare's pencil drew, all the masterstrokes are new'. British theatre in the late nineteenth and early twentieth century cut Shakespeare radically, not because actor-managers believed audiences would not understand the language or would be bored at the complexities of the plot, but in order to facilitate the fashion for elaborate visual spectacle. The stage settings for Shakespeare were highly elaborate affairs that set out to re-create, with as much historical accuracy as possible, the original setting for the action. For example, archaeologists were employed to check that the details of the Roman plays were historically correct. Such realistic settings were expensive to construct, took a great deal of time and labour to change, and, therefore, were changed *only* when the action made it absolutely unavoidable.

Norman Marshall, in *The Producer and the Play*, gives a wonderful example of just what could be done to Shakespeare's text if a determined assault were made on it by the demands of spectacular staging:

He [Augustin Daly, manager of Her Majesty's Theatre] began with the first scene of the second act [of Shakespeare's *Twelfth Night*] – the landing of Antonio and Sebastian. 'This rearrangement,' explained one of the critics, 'although it destroys all dramatic suspense as to the fate of Viola's brother, has the advantage of allowing the star (Miss Rehan) to enter after the audience is seated.' To make things easier for the scene-shifters, the second scene of the first act was played next. Then the sea-coast scene was got out of the way and the Duke's palace was revealed, a fine, elaborate set – so elaborate that there it had to stay for the rest of the act. Daly got out of this difficulty by what one critic described as 'a bold rearrangement of the text'. The first and fourth scenes of Act I were played consecutively as a single scene; then, after the curtain had been lowered for a moment to denote a passage of time, scenes three and five of Act I were joined together with the second scene of Act II, all run together without a break. (p. 157)

Not everyone in the nineteenth-century theatre industry was happy with the appetite of audiences for lavish spectacular presentations loosely based on Shakespeare, and there was a determined effort by some to correct what they saw as an imbalance between spoken language and visual display. But, despite the pioneering work of men such as William Poel, who attempted to re-stage Shakespeare in the context of the Elizabethan theatre – using no elaborate scenery, minimal cutting and allowing the action to flow without having to pause to change the setting – for most of the nineteenth century, in Britain at least, Shakespeare's text was generally subservient to that of actor and designer. His name certainly carried less theatrical weight and lent less status to performance than it does today. Although by the end of the nineteenth century there was a fledgling company which concentrated on playing Shakespeare in his home town of Stratford-upon-Avon, it carried nothing like the status, and attracted only a fraction of the funding and attention that the RSC manages 100 years later.

The Actor

Unlike directors, who come to study a text having to think not only about all the characters, but also about how they are to be represented on the stage (in what context, using what conventions etc.), an actor approaching a text is usually primarily interested in his or her own role, and with those other characters with whom he or she directly, or indirectly, relates. But, in common with directors and readers of Shakespeare, actors live in the shadows of past performances. They cannot escape trailing behind them a whole cloak of historical associations and attitudes towards not only Shakespeare, but also the role they are about to enact.

As you go into the Royal Shakespeare theatre [at Stratford-upon-Avon] you are faced with twelve-foot high pictures of other actors who have done other performances of your part, and their history and their triumphs loom over you: 'Follow that!' It's like coming to Mecca: the ghosts are all around and the fear of failure is very great.

(Zoe Wannamaker, *Players of Shakespeare, Vol. II*, pp. 81–2)

Although there have been some celebrated attempts to break with the directorcratic structure of organizations like the RSC (notably Kenneth Branagh's Renaissance Theatre Company), on the whole, actors exercise very little power or control over the production process. The process of text-into-performance undertaken by directors in many ways parallels that of the active reader and scholar. Indeed, although there is no recognized training in Britain for theatre directors, most of them have been trained to deal with ideas. Consequently, whilst we may feel relatively at home in discussing the role of the modern director, that of the modern actor is more likely to remain mysterious; certainly the actor's preparation is often very different to that of the director. First and foremost, creating a role in a Shakespeare play, or almost any other play, does not always require intellectual/analytical skills. This is not to suggest that actors need never analyse their role or the play as a whole, but their path takes a different route from that of the director. As the actress Janet Suzman remarked:

... *talking about acting* is a contradiction in terms. Gesture, tones of voice, expressions in the eye, movements of the body, all these are quite beyond me to describe in words. ('Hedda Gabler: the Play in Performance' in *Essays in Celebration of the 150th Anniversary of Henrik Ibsen's Birth* (ed. Errol Durbach, p. 83)

Cicely Berry is the voice coach for the RSC and also occasionally directs for them. In working closely with actors she takes a very different approach from most directors:

What interests me is the actual *physical* nature of the text. When we talk, we rather think of it as being mainly to do with our heads. But language evolved from sounds we made to communicate our needs, and that's a very physical thing. We can still be upset by words, they can have a physical effect on us which goes beyond simply how we're thinking.   (RSC *News*, Spring 1985, p. 3)

The active reader of Shakespeare trying to come to terms with the way of the actor, has to start by recognizing that acting is not necessarily seen by actors as a primarily intellectual, or even self-analytical, activity. Many of them will tell you that too much conscious thought about a character, too much 'intellectualizing', can actually become a barrier between the actor's own personality and that of the character he or she is seeking to become. I am aware, having used the word 'become' in that context, that there are other ways of approaching a role that are more concerned with demonstrating or showing rather than 'becoming' a character, but they are outside the mainstream tradition of British theatre where the conventions of illusionism dominate staging, and psychological naturalism dominates acting. Actors are taught not to look at the whole play, at ideas, issues and contradictions that are raised by it, but, instead, are taught to create characters. In this process the surrender of self to the character being portrayed is more valued than a self-conscious awareness of the mechanics of the process the actor is engaged in manufacturing. Audiences, too, are schooled to watch characters rather than to appreciate the craft of acting as such. Those actors who succeed in impersonating characters most convincingly are the most highly rewarded by their profession.

The anti-illusionist approach has a marginal presence in British theatre in general, and is almost entirely absent in productions of Shakespeare. In a book written by the actor Simon Callow it is a director – William Gaskill – who is left to articulate the positive value of a more self-consciously analytical approach to the enactment of a role, while Callow defends what he sees as the legitimacy of an *emotional* identification of the actor with his or her character:

We argued especially about character. It was my deep conviction that all acting is rooted in character. It was a semi-Stanislavskian point of view, but mainly derived from the misery that I experienced as an actor until I had a firm grip on who I was in the play. Bill Gaskill counters by saying that character was a bourgeois concept based on identification. He said that for him who a character was was of no interest, only what he did. These discussions drove me back to the Messingkauf Dialogues of Brecht, which I now understand for the first time. If a play, says Brecht, is a report on an event, the audience only needs to know as much about the characters of the play as makes the event clear. I could see the force of that; but I knew in my heart exactly what kind of performances I liked to see.   (*Being an Actor*, p. 62)

What contribution, then, can the reader-as-actor make to the debate of text-into-performance, which must, of course, be conducted as an analytical exercise, for it is no good telling an examiner that, for example, you wanted to play Lady Macbeth as a contemporary 'bag' lady because in your heart it 'felt' right! Unless you can argue for your reading of a part then you are likely to be in trouble. This still means recognizing and accepting that an actor's part in the rehearsal debate may not always be expressed orally. An actor makes meaning and articulates feelings through the whole body: through gestures, tone of voice and an intuitive sense of what *feels* right or true. Our theatrical culture values words and operates a convention of performance which imitates reality. However, non-verbal means of communication used consciously and unconsciously by actors are always important aspects of any performance. The text being articulated by an actor sometimes owes as much to intuition or an unconscious adherence to convention as it does to the actor's intellect. It is difficult, therefore, for a reader to emulate the actor's approach to his or her text (we *have* to use words to express our ideas about the text), but we can, and should, none the less, acknowledge that an actor's view of a character, and the questions that need to be asked, are often very different from those that tend to occupy a director.

Some actors will attempt to research a character by approaching it, as it were, from the inside out. They adopt the methods of a psychological detective, attempting to get inside the head of the character and look at the world of the play through his or her eyes. Most contemporary actors adopt such techniques of psychological naturalism that have their origins in the teachings of the Russian director Konstantin Stanislavsky. Daniel Massey, the Duke in Adrian Noble's 1983 RSC production of *Measure for Measure*, writes:

I used my own personal psychological journey to heighten the dramatic tension of that opening sequence [Act I, scene i]. I was able to identify very deeply with what we felt were the Duke's problems ... A gesture as immense as handing

over the reins of power to a young and relatively inexperienced Angelo must go
hand-in-hand, I felt, with some sort of psychological crisis.

(Players of Shakespeare, Vol. II, p. 17)

There are actors who take a different approach. They come at their
roles, as it were, from the outside in. For example, an actor may choose
a particular physical characteristic such as Richard III's deformity,
or, in the case of Laurence Olivier's performance of Othello, the actor's
initial concern began with the voice and movements of a black
nobleman. According to his book, *Year of the King*, Antony Sher's
performance of Richard III owed much to his detailed and painstaking
preparation for the role. He spent a lot of time observing people in
institutions with severe mental and physical handicaps. The point is
that actors, students and scholars do not necessarily share the same
approach to Shakespeare. The readers who attempt to put themselves
in the position of an actor will need to adjust their conventional analytical approach to the text, but, in doing so, they will learn a lot that
might otherwise have been missed. For, if you wanted to actually play
Hamlet it would not be a requirement demanded of your agent by the
producers that, at your audition, you could demonstrate a knowledge
of current critical thinking on the play. But, it would be expected that,
as an actor, you would try to discover (and this is what an active reader
can also do) how the other characters think and feel about him, and, of
course, how he thinks and feels about himself.

If you want to try to reproduce the actor's process of making a text,
when you read a play remember to draw a distinction between what
you know, given your overview of the play as a whole, and what your
particular character or characters *can* know, given their limited knowledge of the events and issues of the play as a whole. For example,
when Hamlet goes off on his enforced journey to England, the actor
playing the role is off-stage for some considerable time. It is, therefore,
important to remember that if you are thinking as if you were the actor
playing Hamlet, you must exclude from your thoughts about the character any material that takes place during his absence about which Hamlet
cannot be aware, and subsequently does not learn. Of course, in the
Elizabethan theatre, when the actors were not given the whole play to
study, simply their own roles, what happened to their characters, and
to those with whom they interacted, would have necessarily been their
only concern.

Silent Characters

Not all actors, especially young and inexperienced ones, get to speak

Shakespeare when they first learn about performing him in public. When thinking about actors and about how they approach the task of playing Shakespeare, remember, as a first principle, that any actor on stage being observed by an audience *is* acting, irrespective of whether or not he or she happens to be speaking. The significance of this simple fact (that acting is more than talking) is sometimes forgotten when reading a dramatist's text. Indeed, whenever we are studying the manufacturing process of text-into-performance it is necessary to remember that the dramatic significance of a character cannot automatically be measured by the number of words he or she is given to speak. The active reader must try to recall and visualize the totality of events which act and react upon one another to produce the context in which words are understood.

An important part of actors' training is teaching them the importance not only of speaking, but also of being able to listen. The enactment of listening in a performance text can be of equal, if not greater, significance to an expressive act like talking. Take, for example, the relationship between Hamlet and Horatio, or that between Rosalind and Celia in *As You Like It*. In both plays there is little doubt as to which of the two friends has ultimately the most responsibility for carrying the play's meaning, but, if we want to understand either play, it is not enough to study, however assiduously, only the words spoken by Hamlet or Rosalind. It is often also necessary to construct Horatio's or Celia's *response* to what is said; for, although neither has as much dialogue, there are frequent occasions when both are on-stage at the same time as their more voluble partners, and when they are being talked to, or when they are being ignored, their presence in the scene helps to shape the way in which the audience understands it. When Hamlet speaks, he often is speaking his thoughts aloud (in soliloquy). Sometimes it appears as if he is directly addressing the audience, but sometimes, too, he is addressing another character, and when he does, the addressee generates a text through his or her responses to what Hamlet says. That reaction, generated through body language, may well influence what Hamlet says and, in particular, the *way* in which he says it. Although Hamlet is speaking the Shakespeare text you can *read*, Horatio, or who ever else it may be, is just as significantly articulating a response that the reader needs to see (and to invent) in the theatre of the mind's eye if the totality of the exchange is to be completed. As far as an audience watching the play in performance are concerned, neither Hamlet, nor any other single character, is speaking *the* text, because that is what the audience themselves are making by observing

57

the activity of the actors in a dramatic context, and making something significant out of it.

An illustration of this aspect of making a performance text is provided in Act Four, scene one of *As You Like It*. Suppose the dialogue between Rosalind and Orlando is overheard by a third character, as it is this scene when Celia is the silent but expressive witness to the love games taking place in the Forest of Arden. To the casual reader, Celia's role may not be immediately clear; her presence may even be forgotten entirely and, because she has few lines to speak, you may be tempted to dismiss her potential dramatic significance. But, any director of the scene, as well as the actress playing the role, and certainly any active reader, has to decide *how* Celia reacts. Does she approve or disapprove of the conduct of her friend? Does she find their behaviour amusing, or embarrassing? Her witness to this private act makes it public ... do, therefore, Rosalind and Orlando recognize the presence of an audience and 'play' for Celia? Or do they ignore her? The permutations are almost endless, but they must be resolved in one way or another. If Celia's, or any other character's presence on-stage is indicated by the printed text, then the active reader can't ignore him or her. *You* may have to decide, if that character is visible to the audience, whether or not he or she is visible to other characters. Can this character overhear what is being said by someone else, and is that speaker's text modified in any way as a result? How does this silent, but expressive, character react to what he or she sees and hears? Does his or her reaction further condition the text of the audience, and if so, in what way?

The difficulty in taking sufficient account of the influence of so-called silent characters on the construction of meaning is made more problematic in Shakespeare than it is in the work of many other dramatists. Readers coming to study the plays for public examinations are rightly reminded by their teachers of the need to pay attention to the beauty, complexity and poetic quality of the language. But, Shakespeare was not only, or even primarily, a poet, he was a dramatist, and however beautiful his words may be they cannot be fully understood without the context in which they are spoken being supplied in real or imagined performance. This is daunting for some readers because it inevitably puts them consciously into a creative and active relationship with the text. Essentially you are acknowledging consciously what subconsciously you always knew: the printed text is incomplete, and a combination of your imagination and intellect is going to complete it. What is said in performance, and what is meant, do not always correspond.

When reading Shakespeare (or any dramatist) the reader's focus of attention is almost invariably and understandably drawn to the words being spoken by what seem to be the principal actors in the drama, but as we have already noted, you cannot necessarily judge the dramatic significance of an actor's role simply by concentrating on what he or she actually says. Further exploration of the role of actors who appear to have very little to say demonstrates the fruitfulness of considering the function of so-called 'silent characters'.

If we go back to the wooing scene in *Richard III*, we will find a good example of the potential dramatic power of silent characters to articulate a text, and of the need for the active reader to take positive interpretative decisions to facilitate an enactment of the whole text and not just that part of it represented by the words spoken by the leading players. This scene is a classic case of action that cannot be fully comprehended by the reader unless that reader is prepared to activate his or her theatrical imagination and take up the creative challenge offered by it.

In *Richard III* the following direction appears:

Enter the corse of Henry the Sixth, with halberds to guard it; Lady Anne being the mourner.

Now, the corpse of the dead king (played presumably by an actor and not by a dummy) cannot walk on to the stage, and it will therefore need to be carried by at least six actors. The directions specify that the corpse is guarded; it therefore seems reasonable to suppose that those who carry the body of the dead king are in no position to guard it, and that we therefore require another group of actors to enact the guard. You must decide how many guards guard the funeral procession of a dead king. Shakespeare himself may have been thinking of the historical evidence contained in Edward Hall's *The Union of the Noble and Illustre Famelies of Lancastre and York*, published in 1548. In this history the funeral of Henry VI is described as a poor affair:

> without Priest or Clarke, Torche or Taper,
> syngyn or saiyng . . .

Given this, and the relatively small numbers of actors employed by an Elizabethan company, plus the fact that Lady Anne is the only person of rank and status in society to be present, let us suppose that there are six halberds to guard the corpse (not many when you think of state funerals). Although the opening directions don't refer to them, two characters are mentioned by name in the subsequent spoken text: Tressel and Berkeley. These two gentlemen enter with the funeral procession, making a cast of at least sixteen actors on-stage at the beginning of the scene: six pall-bearers, six halberds guarding the corpse, Lady Anne, Tressel and Berkeley, and the corpse of Henry VI. When the actor playing Richard enters the scene, you have a stage crowded with seventeen actors, and a printed text that is apparently only concerned with two.

Having noted the number of actors required for this scene, you now have to consider their significance. How do they enter the playing-area, and what impression are you seeking to communicate to an audience by your handling of that entry? At this point all *I* can do is what I hope *you* will also do – but for yourself, in your own terms that is – begin to animate the text.

Let us say that the procession is formal and solemn. There is no music to accompany the entrance, and the very silence creates an air of expectancy and concentration on this strange sight. Tressel and Berkeley lead the way, followed by the corpse held shoulder-high and closely surrounded by the guards. Lady Anne follows in the rear. It is important to make clear to the audience that it is she alone who is responsible for this funeral rite of a dead king. The corpse is heavy, and the progress slow. The group of actors take their time in progressing across the stage. They give the audience time to both note the solemnity of the occasion, and also to register that the control and responsibility rests with the only woman on-stage: it is she who begins the spoken text with a command to, 'Set down, set down your honourable load.' As the body of Henry is referred to by Lady Anne throughout the scene, and indeed is used by her as her only defence against the onslaught of Richard's rhetoric, its position on-stage is important. The corpse ought to be physically, as it is metaphorically, central to the action of what follows. The actor playing the corpse is one of the silent characters, but throughout the scene he reminds the audience of what Richard has done in the very recent past, and of the nature of the occasion on which he has chosen to do his 'wooing'.

At Anne's command to set down the corpse, the bearers, guards, and Tressel and Berkeley cease to have active roles to play in the proceedings and become passive spectators. They are an on-stage audience which begins to witness Anne's fulfilment of her role in this spectacle: the formal lamentation of 'virtuous Lancaster'. The presence of fifteen men gives this lament a public quality, and as a public act, a required performance, it carries with it the stress of responsibility for appropriate behaviour. Up to and including this lament, Lady Anne is controlling the progress of the ritual, but immediately Richard enters the stage, this control is lost, never to be regained. He takes over events, and directs and manipulates them according to his own design. Even before he enters, the authority of Anne is undermined and she is seen as uncertain and tentative. She gives an order to go on, only to countermand it seconds later:

> Come now, towards Chertsey with your holy load,
> Taken from Paul's to be interrèd there.
> And still, as you are weary of this weight,
> Rest you, whiles I lament King Henry's corse.
>
> (lines 29–32)

Richard's entry is so well timed, coming as it does when the bearers are caught with the heavy corpse on their shoulders, uncertain whether to go on or stay, that he may well have been observing the events (visible to the audience perhaps) and waiting for his opportunity. When he intervenes, the bearers are not sure what to do. Anne has told them to take their 'holy load' up again and, even as they are doing so, orders them to 'rest'. Richard's opening line, 'Stay, you that bear the corse, and set it down', is spoken as if to intervene on Anne's behalf. It is as if Richard has taken over responsibility for the scene's ritual, and once this has demonstrably happened, Anne's control of events is critically weakened, just as her self-control will be undermined by Richard's actions. The formality of the funeral ritual, where all concerned know what to do and what to expect, instantly disappears with the arrival of Richard, and Lady Anne is denied the relative sense of security and comfort that comes from her participation in a scenario that is known and familiar. Those who, together with her, were a part of a ritual and had specific supporting roles to play (the fifteen men who accompany the corpse), are equally suddenly denied their role and their joint purpose is replaced by individual uncertainty about how to act. Instead of participants, they become observers. As such, their presence on-stage during the subsequent action reminds the audience in the theatre that collectively they have the physical power to intervene, but lack the will to do so.

Richard controls events through fear of what he might do, rather than through what he does, or even of what he is realistically capable of doing. What happens to Lady Anne is shocking, yet understandable, if seen in performance. It is akin to a nightmare in which a victim cries out for help, and although help is all around, it fails to materialize into action. Anne's seduction, or, as I prefer to think of it, her molestation by Richard, is witnessed by two equally helpless sets of spectators. Throughout the entire running time of this extraordinarily theatrical scene, only two lines are actually spoken by anyone other than Richard and Lady Anne, yet what they say, and its significance, can be understood by the reader only if he or she is prepared to recognize the role being played by the silent, but far from inconsequential, characters on-stage with them.

What I have suggested above in order to bring that scene to life is not, of course, *the* way to interpret what takes place, but it is *a* way of coming to terms with what to do with actors whom Shakespeare indicates are present, but does not clearly state why. My interpretation of this scene can quite easily be turned on its head. Let us suppose that the actress playing Lady Anne understands her character to be not someone weak and vulnerable, but a calculating mature woman who was never particularly close to her father-in-law and who is merely fulfilling a public duty which cannot be avoided. Furthermore, that actress may see Anne as shallow and power-hungry, and suppose her initial response to Richard to be only a sham because she is secretly pleased and flattered by the attentions of one so close to real political power. In this interpretation, Anne cannot behave other than as she does because the presence of the other on-stage characters monitoring her speech and actions, makes the occasion one in which it is necessary for her to present an appropriate public face. My point is that when you are reading, they, and other silent characters, cannot and should not be ignored. If they are there, then the reader must consciously make interpretative decisions as to what to do with them.

The potential significance of silent characters needs to be recognized by the active reader and their presence in the action of the performance text animated in the reader's imagination.

Gesture

We have already seen that actors use more than the spoken word to compose their performance texts. Physical gesture is a very important part of our everyday body language used, often unconsciously, to communicate with others. A couple who walk together holding hands are obviously signalling for all to see that they are literally, as well as emotionally, connected, or tied to each other. It is an exclusive gesture which precludes other people. Nodding at someone as you pass them in the street as opposed to waving or blowing a kiss, would indicate to a casual spectator different levels of familiarity. The complicated language and vocabulary of gesture was more sophisticated and codified in Elizabethan England than it is now. Then, many people were illiterate but more used than we are to reading the signs contained in gestural language. The American Shakespearean editor and scholar, David Bevington, reminds us that on the Elizabethan stage,

Kneeling, embracing, clasping of hands, bowing, removing the hat, assuming a proper place at table, deferring to others in going through a doorway – all are part of a rich vocabulary expressing contractual obligations, obedience, homage, submission, fealty, petition, hospitality, parental authority, royal prerogative.

(*Action is Eloquence*, p. 136)

Bevington also makes the important point that,

the very familiarity of such gestures generates also a language of nuance by means of which Elizabethan spectators might recognize, through subtle variations from the norm, signals of estrangement, defiance of authority, and other kinds of social inversion. (Ibid., p. 153)

If you are used to being regularly saluted with a nod or wave from a passing acquaintance you may think nothing of it, and take it for granted until the day when the acquaintance *fails* to conform to the established code of behaviour by ignoring you entirely. Then, the *absence* of the gesture becomes highly significant. A good example of how this can work in performances of Shakespeare is the one cited by Bevington, in *Richard II*. Richard returns from a military campaign in Ireland to find Bolingbroke and his followers in revolt against the Crown. In Act Three, scene three, outside the walls of Flint Castle, Bolingbroke speaks throughout Richard's entrance on to the walls of the castle. As Bolingbroke becomes aware of Richard's presence the audience become aware of who, if anyone, is now kneeling in the presence of their lawful king. Those who do kneel (and there are some who do not), are instantly registered and thus graphically communicate to the audience the reality of the division in the land. Buckingham stays upright; this failure to observe the traditional form of public acknowledgement of the sovereign's power and authority (he is made, literally, higher than everyone else) makes for a powerful visual metaphor. The contradictory responses and the significance of the brief tableau is not lost on Richard, a king for whom the rituals of kingship are of paramount significance:

> We are amazed; and thus long have we stood
> To watch the fearful bending of thy knee,
> Because we thought ourself thy lawful king.
> And if we be, how dare thy joints forget
> To pay their awful duty to our presence?
>
> (lines 72–6)

You can see from that last quotation that, in this case, the printed text itself contains the evidence required to establish the existence and significance in performance of a particular gesture.

Minor Characters

If they are fortunate, young actors playing silent characters in Shakespeare may also be given a few lines to speak when asked to play a so-called minor character. When reading Shakespeare's plays, and, in particular, when reading the tragedies, it is possible to get caught up in an almost obsessive way with the great acting roles around which the texts are built. Until very recently there was a marked critical tendency to discuss some of the plays, for instance *Hamlet* and *Macbeth*, as if they were *only* concerned with Hamlet and Macbeth. But, the tragedies can be constructed in performance to explore not only the individual psychology of their leading protagonists, but also to explore political and social issues, and to highlight contradictions in ideology, race and gender. Anyone interested in reading Shakespeare with a view to constructing a real or imagined performance has got to take account of all the characters, and not simply those who have been given the most words to speak. So-called minor characters may be used in order to create a major dramatic impact. These roles may not attract the attention of more conventional modes of literary analysis but may be of enormous significance in performance. As a way of approaching Shakespeare's text from the position of an actor, go through the list of characters, and temporarily discard all the names you immediately recognize. Those you are left with will almost always repay the time you spend considering their possible function. Let us look, as an example, at two such roles listed amongst the characters in *Macbeth*, but given no more than a footnote in most critical commentaries: a Doctor and a Gentlewoman.

This pair actually appear together in one of the most famous scenes in all of Shakespeare: the sleepwalking scene (V, i). If you are familiar with this scene, what you probably know about it is bound up with an image in your mind of Lady Macbeth, vulnerable, alone, and very close to death. But, the scene opens with the presence on stage of the Doctor and Gentlewoman who wait for Lady Macbeth to enter. Their waiting, and what they have to say and do, prepares the audience for what they are about to witness. The audience learn that the two have waited before, and that Lady Macbeth has been seen to walk in her sleep. The enactment of sleepwalking is not a common occurrence on the Elizabethan or Jacobean stage, and Shakespeare uses the presence of these minor characters in part to ensure instant recognition of the signals given out by the actress playing Lady Macbeth. For this reason, the opening fifteen lines of the scene begin that process of preparation.

When the actress enters, she is immediately identified by the Gentle-woman (remember when Lady Macbeth was last seen she was wearing a costume which instantly identified her as a queen, and now she appears in a nightgown): 'Lo you! Here she comes. This is her very guise.' What the audience see in the silent performance of the actress playing Lady Macbeth is verbally reinforced by the commentary, 'upon my life, fast asleep'. The Doctor and Gentlewoman then proceed to draw the atten-tion of the audience to her hand in which she holds a lighted taper, a particularly potent and powerful symbol in this play. They ensure that the audience begin to grasp that its significance is more than practical: 'She has light by her *continually*' (author's italics). All the subsequent actions of Lady Macbeth in this, her last scene in the play, are com-mented upon by the Doctor and Gentlewoman in order that the audi-ence are guided towards a recognition of the true significance of Lady Macbeth's silent actions. These two minor characters function as a chorus in this scene. They also have another major task: they help the audience to empathize with Lady Macbeth's self-inflicted hurt. Both characters are recognizable as caring – the Doctor for the health of the body, the Gentlewoman for the day-to-day needs of Lady Macbeth. Yet, despite being literally, and symbolically, close to her, neither can render any assistance or relief from distress. Together, those minor characters introduce the important idea of the threat that exists to the mortal soul of Lady Macbeth. She is seen guarding a small light of conscience, but that light is extremely vulnerable and liable to go out at any moment. Her eventual suicide would have been seen by the original audience as a tragedy, not least because suicide was believed to be a mortal sin, entailing the loss of eternal life. However, the audience have been prepared, and their comprehension of the action of the scene shaped, by the interjections and commentary provided by the Doctor and Gentlewoman. They speak of heaven, prayer, and God, and of the need for this confession (for confession is what Lady Macbeth's com-pulsive walking really is) to be heard by a priest, who can offer absolu-tion and forgiveness, rather than by two people (and a whole theatre of others) who can offer only sympathy.

There are, then, no minor characters. You could argue that some are more marginal than others, but in Shakespeare in particular, that is an argument likely to lead you away from comprehending how the perform-ance text works. In your study of his plays, and also those of other dramatists, never regard a character as superfluous, however little he or she may be given to say, or however infrequent his or her appearances on stage.

The Visual Text

There has always been a certain tension in the theatre between the demands of the visual text to be seen, and those of the spoken word to be heard. For some people, Shakespeare has always been a poet first and a dramatist second. The former prefer to read a play rather than see it performed; the beauty and complexity of the language are quite sufficient. Presumably, this was a disposition shared by the creator of the BBC's long-running radio programme *Desert Island Discs*; awaiting the lucky castaway on the island is a convenient copy of the complete works, which, together with eight discs, the Bible and a book of the castaway's own choosing, is there to 'while away a dreary hour twixt breakfast and supper time'. Shakespeare is there as a *literary* text (it is a *radio* programme), the plays aren't on video, and they won't be performed by the desert island's resident classical repertory company. But, despite the Bard's reputation as a literary genius, most people probably appreciate the plays most when they experience them as performances made for the theatre, for television or for the cinema. And because of the nature of all three of these media, the visual and spoken texts are of equal significance to audiences. They should also be *equally* significant to the reader of Shakespeare. However, the visual texts created by the grouping of actors, their individual and collective language of gestures, their costumes and the totality of the environment (the stage design) in which they are seen and understood, has generally received relatively little critical attention in comparison to that given the written or spoken text.

In performance, Shakespeare's company of actors *combined* the visual and spoken text in order to construct meanings: the visual text was certainly not considered inferior to dialogue by the Elizabethan audience. In what was a largely pre-literate age, they were schooled to acknowledge that truth could be apprehended in images, and all action accordingly unfolded through a combination of dialogue, movement and gesture, pageantry and symbolism.

The Designer

The role of the stage designer, like that of the director, is a relatively modern innovation. Shakespeare's theatre would not have employed an individual to create a specific environment for acting any more than one employed to tell actors how to act. However, since the nineteenth century, the role of the stage designer, like that of the director, has become increasingly important, and, today, no reader of Shakespeare can read the plays without, consciously or unconsciously, designing a setting in which the words on the page are understood. The task that faces a designer, or, in our case, a reader attempting to consciously construct a designer's visual text from Shakespeare's printed one, is principally to create an appropriate environment for acting, and in doing so, to recognize that what is created can never be neutral. Decisions about the use of the playing space made by the actors, and the relationship of that space to the audience are, essentially, part of stage design. From the minute the given environment or 'setting' for the actors is seen by an audience, it will be transmitting signals to them; signals they may or may not be consciously aware of receiving, but which, none the less, act together with others generated in different but complementary ways (for example, through words, gestures, costumes, properties, lighting, sound and so on) to manufacture *meaning* in the performance text. A designer's text, like a performer's, is capable of articulating meanings and creating mood and atmosphere.

Until quite recently the presentation of Shakespeare in Britain was almost entirely concerned with communicating ideas or concepts that had arisen either as part of a lengthy rehearsal process or, more frequently, had occurred to the director in his or her pre-production study of the text. Although this academic approach arose as a result of a close study of the language of the play, it was none the less considered desirable and appropriate by many directors to see it as part of their role to find stage designers capable of articulating those ideas on the stage in visual terms. For example, in a celebrated production of *Richard II*, directed by John Barton for the RSC in 1974, Barton decided to alternate the two leading actors in the roles of Richard and Bolingbroke. He did this in order to facilitate the exploration of what he saw as Richard's 'compulsive role-playing'. He also had to find a designer sympathetic to his ideas about how to stage the play. He finally chose Timothy O'Brien and Tazeena Firth. O'Brien subsequently wrote:

The designer had these thoughts in trying to present the play: first there was the fact of the alternating leading players in the context of an acting company; secondly there was the idea of Richard II as a compulsive role-player; thirdly, the sense that the play was like a bad dream with its central figures wandering

without remedy towards certain destruction; and lastly, the great challenge of
the play to a designer, the upper level at Flint Castle.   (see 'Designing a
Shakespeare Play: Richard II', *Deutsches Gesellschaft (West) Jahrbuch*,
Heidelberg, 1974)

Despite what O'Brien saw as the 'great challenge' for the designer, it is
noticeable that he none the less foregrounds the director's ideas, and
sees his own role primarily as having to create an appropriate and
comprehensible language of symbols which will express the director's
interpretation of the printed text in performance.

In the days leading up to the beginning of rehearsals, directors and
designers usually meet frequently to discuss the forthcoming production
and how it is to look. By the time the actors start to be included in the
process, the design of the stage on which they will act, and the costumes
they will be expected to wear, will almost always have been decided; a
scale model of the set will usually be displayed when all the cast meet
together for the first time at the 'read through'.

Like Shakespeare's Richard II, all of us are continually bound up in
the business of self-presentation, and that frequently means acting like
a stage designer. For, just as we continually design what we hope is an
appropriate appearance for ourselves by choosing what to wear in
public, we also attempt, as we saw when we discussed casting in the
previous chapter, to 'read' other people from their external appearance.
Equally, we create a personal space, such as a bedroom or study, not
only to make it comfortable, but also with half an eye on the reactions
of anyone else who might be invited to see it. A few minutes in the
house of a new acquaintance, particularly if he or she is absent for long
enough to let us take a good look round, will provide a lot of information from which to make at least some tentative assumptions about his
or her class, character and lifestyle. The fact that the signs may be
misleading and sometimes appear contradictory does not stop the impulse to decipher them. Indeed, people generally encourage such speculation by designing the interior of their homes in such a way as to make a
statement about themselves and what they value. You might, for example, look to see if a house you are visiting has any books or records,
and if so, how many and of what kind. Are there any pictures on the
walls? Is the house tidy? Is it so clean as to make you feel uncomfort-
able? All these and many more impressions go to make up the 'feel' of
the place. Obviously, the impressions are no more than that, and can be
misleading. They may also not be interpreted in the same way by
different observers. To some, the presence in the living room of a huge
television and the absence of any books will be a negative signal indicat-

ing, at best, some cultural deprivation; to others, it may be a welcome sign of possible future access to superior viewing facilities. Whatever the environment, it is difficult to entirely divorce an individual from the setting in which he or she chooses to be seen. Learning to read *that* setting or design involves consciously decoding the signals it gives out, instead of simply being subconsciously influenced by them.

In fact, people today are relatively sophisticated at manufacturing and decoding visual texts of their own. We certainly cannot escape being influenced, at least subconsciously, by carefully contrived images that flow continually from the advertising industry. But as students of text-into-performance we can learn a lot from advertising about how images are constructed in order to contain coded messages to be subsequently decoded by the targeted audience. If we begin to acquire the rudiments of semiotics (the language of signs), our ability to 'read' not just an advertisement, but also performances of Shakespeare in the theatre, on film, television *and* in the imagination, will be enhanced. We will also have the chance to acquire a vocabulary that is used in all forms of performance art.

One form of television advertising with which most of us are familiar is the party political broadcast. The anonymous designers of these images (and presumably also those who appear in them) believe that the visual text they are creating is a powerful force in influencing an audience to think and act (by voting) in a certain way. Like all advertising, party political broadcasts are a form of theatre containing an environment which is richly coded and full of carefully designed and controlled images. When party leaders or spokespersons are seen, great care will usually have been taken to ensure that their immediate environment is appropriate to the image intended to be projected. The setting for the filming is invariably illusionistic; the viewer does not see the studio, the film crew, the make-up team, etc., everything that appears on the screen has been made to look spontaneous and real, the mediation of reality is heavily disguised.

It is a common complaint that the strategy of political-campaign managers is to create, via political images for transmission by the mass media, a product designed to sell the *personality* of the leader, rather than to explain the policies of the party he or she represents. Often, he or she is seen alone (although, of course, in reality the speaker is surrounded by an unseen film crew, advisors, etc.) in a room containing lots of books. The viewer can't make out any titles, but they look weighty (literally), and are generally expensively bound – certainly never paperbacks! The books are there in the background as part of an overall design which is meant to signal to the audience that their owner is both educated, and has immediate access to information and knowledge. You might have thought that the modern politician would have wanted to indicate the latter by having a computer screen on a desk or table close by, but, operating such a machine has too many associations with the lowly task of a typist, and is therefore usually avoided. What concerns the makers of the image is the centrality of symbols that convey traditional values and attitudes. On a nearby desk or table is invariably a vase of flowers. The flowers have to be chosen with care, but they are there to suggest a certain affluence and elegance, the 'green' credentials of the politician, and, also, to hint that he or she is sensitive to the natural world, and possesses an aesthetic sensibility. Indeed, flowers can be used as an image for a particular party, as in the case of the British Labour party's adoption of the red rose (an image borrowed from the successful election campaign of President Mitterrand in France). The flowers, plus perhaps one or two photographs (the preference, as in American Presidential broadcasts, is for children), suggest the existence of a 'homely', 'domestic' side to the personality of the person seeking power and control over the rest of us: despite their real or desired exalted status, the message runs, they remain in touch with ordinary day-to-day domestic life.

The architecture of the setting is also important and carries messages. Walls are sometimes wood-panelled, suggesting permanence and antiquity. Panelling also hints at a study, or an ancient seat of learning, thus lending to its (temporary) inhabitant an air of authority, permanence and continuity with the traditions and values of the past. Visiting political figures to the White House in Washington are invariably (at least during the winter months) photographed with the President side-by-side, next to a blazing log fire. Presumably, the White House central heating is not inadequate, but the lure of the image of a cosy fireside chat is an irresistible bait and a splendid 'photo opportunity'.

In party political broadcasts, and in their American counterparts, the furniture will have been carefully selected to complement the other visual elements in the overall design. The whole environment must avoid extreme statements, it must reassure, not provoke. Almost certainly, the final image will not be overtly contemporary. It may be traditional, but never over elaborate or old fashioned.

The individual, or rather the group-interest represented by the individual who is the central focus of the design, must have a personal image which is equally carefully manufactured. Hair, clothes and posture are given a great deal of thought. Seated figures rarely sit back in a chair, but sit upright, ready to respond immediately to any urgent call; the desired impression is of an alert, not simply a relaxed stance, and the designer has to avoid suggesting too much comfort attached to the role in which the individual is supposed to be *working* on behalf of the viewer.

The camera-work will be subtle, usually focusing on the upper body and, especially, the face of the party spokesperson. The lighting will be soft and the whole image lit in such a way as to flatter rather than to reveal the subject.

When you come to read a play by Shakespeare, or any other dramatist, as if you were a potential director or actor, and certainly when you try to read it through the perspective of a designer, it is very important to be able to locate the action taking place in your imagination to the given dimensions and conditions of a real playing space. From experience gained from going to the theatre you may decide to draw on your familiarity with a whole range of very different kinds of theatre spaces, ranging from small, crowded and hot rooms in public houses, seating no more than fifty in varying degrees of discomfort, to huge purpose-built, air-conditioned auditoria seating upwards of 1000 spectators. Such very different kinds of environment for acting establish particular kinds of audience/performer relationships. They may also influence the theatrical conventions governing the staging of plays within them. For example, in a studio theatre such as the RSC's The Pit, which seats only a couple of hundred people who often surround the actors on four sides and are seldom more than a few feet away from them, a minimalist acting style has developed similar to that used in television and film. The audience tend to focus attention on the face of the actor, especially on the eyes and mouth. So close are they to the action, and so intimate is the space being shared with the actors, that the latter fear an accusation of falseness or even of being called 'hams' if their facial gestures and vocal range are not judged sufficiently 'natural'. But, in a large auditorium it is not possible for an actor to speak as if he or she were in a living room and hope to be heard in the gallery, let alone the back of the stalls. Also, any gesture that is meant to be recognized and noted has to be correspondingly magnified in a larger theatre. Arguably, a small space tends to suit plays such as *Othello* and *Macbeth* with a strong domestic theme, both of which have recently received notably successful performances in studio conditions,

71

whereas the history cycle, for example, seems to call for the pageantry and display only really possible on a much larger stage.

Whilst at school, college or university you will almost certainly have encountered performances of Shakespeare on film and video and in a wide range of different theatre spaces – from purpose-built studios with flexible seating, to converted rooms and ill-equipped stages in school halls. Indeed, there is a growing awareness amongst performers and audiences of the potential that exists for an exciting theatrical experience almost anywhere other than on the traditional proscenium-arch stage. You can create an ideal imaginary playing space, which of course will owe a great deal to what you already know about theatres, or altern- atively, you can set the action in the context of the playing conditions enjoyed by Shakespeare's company. Although the task of a designer is to create an environment for acting, he or she has to do so within the limitations of the chosen performance space.

The Elizabethan and Jacobean Performance Space

Despite the vast amount of literature, and the research that has been done on the playing conditions experienced by Elizabethan and Jaco- bean actors and audiences, hard facts are difficult to find and there is still much speculation about them. The recent archaeological discoveries of the foundations of the Globe and Rose theatres on the south bank of the Thames in London may yet tell us more, but, whatever they even- tually reveal, what it was actually like to sit or stand in the Globe watching Shakespeare will always remain somewhat mysterious. Simi- larly, although we know quite a lot about the management of the theatres, the status of actors and the conventions governing perform- ance, we will never know how Burbage played Hamlet, what he sounded and looked like.

Several drawings exist (mostly from contemporary maps) of the ex- terior of the public playhouses on the south bank, but, the only pictorial evidence of what their interiors may have looked like, and, most import- antly from our point of view, what the stage itself was like, comes to us from the famous De Witt drawing of the Swan playhouse which remained undiscovered until the late nineteenth century.

Exciting though it is, there are problems with the De Witt evidence: it poses as many questions as it does answers. We cannot tell, for example, whether the artist was recording a rehearsal or a performance, or whether the drawing was done at the time, or, subsequently, from memory, and so included only those things that appeared to its creator

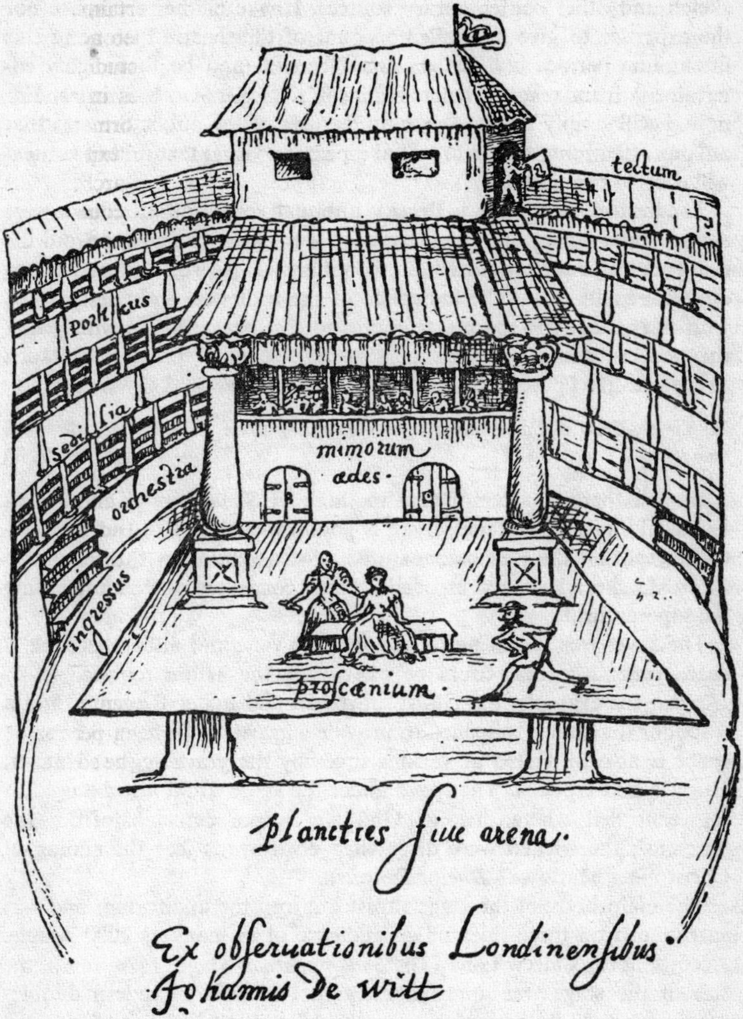

The labels within the drawing read:

tectum

porticus

sedilia

orchestra

mimorum aedes

ingressus

proscenium

planities siue arena.

Ex obseruationibus Londinensibus
Johannis de Witt

De Witt's drawing of the Swan, c. 1596, University Library, Utrecht (Mary Evans
Picture Library)

at the time as being of interest. None the less, there are certain key features of the stage and auditorium which can be deduced from the sketch and other contemporary sources. I have neither the space nor the expertise to give a detailed account of the theatre history of this fascinating period, but readers could benefit (and be thoroughly entertained) from reading Peter Thomson's *Shakespeare's Theatre*. For now, I will simply set out the main features of the public theatres that anyone attempting to create a Shakespearean visual text in that context will need to bear in mind.

The theatres were open to the sky, although some of the audience were seated under cover, and the stage itself was partially shielded from the elements by a roof supported on two pillars which projected out, covering about half of it. The underside of the roof was probably painted with stars, suns and moons, to represent the 'heavens'. It is likely that the 'heavens' could also open to allow the descent of special effects such as the god-like figures required in both *The Tempest* and *Cymbeline*:

Jupiter descends in thunder and lightning, sitting upon an eagle. He throws a thunderbolt. (*Cymbeline*, V, iv)

Although there is a temptation to think of Shakespeare's theatre as technically unsophisticated, there is good evidence – like that above – to suggest that the Elizabethans used all the technology then available to create special effects, especially those connected with representing the supernatural.

The stage was raised up to improve the view and also to provide a space beneath it that could be used when the action required it. In *Hamlet*, for example, the Ghost moves around under the stage, and a trapdoor (or doors) is opened to provide a grave for Ophelia. The same space is also inhabited at various times by the gravediggers, Hamlet, Horatio and Ophelia. The space under the stage could also be used to represent hell where, just as God-like figures descended from the 'heavens', the wicked were dispatched downwards (see the ending of Christopher Marlowe's *Doctor Faustus*).

The main body of the stage thrust out into the auditorium and was surrounded on three sides by an audience of as many as 2000 people. According to Andrew Gurr (*The Shakespearean Stage, 1574–1642*), the size of the stage was approximately that of half a modern doubles tennis-court. At the rear of the stage, and forming a back wall facing the audience, was the tiring-house. Here, the actors waited for their cue to enter, and changed their costumes as the script required. Set into this wall, or wooden façade, were two large doors, these formed the only way of entering or leaving the stage. The tiring-house was probably also the site of the raised, balcony area required in so many of Shakespeare's plays: the balcony in *Romeo and Juliet*; Cleopatra's Monument in *Antony and Cleopatra*; the walls of Flint Castle in *Richard II*, etc. Thus we have three basic acting areas on the Elizabethan public stage: a raised area (the balcony), the flat stage and the under-stage area. It is possible that there was also a fourth so-called 'discovery space' to facilitate such effects as that required in *The Tempest*, where, in Act Five, scene one, Ferdinand and Miranda are 'discovered' playing chess.

These public theatres made an excellent space for the actor (there were, of course, no women performers on the stage until after the theatres reopened at the end of the English Civil War), as he was the focal point of interest. The stage provided the actor with a commanding position, and, at the same time, the audience were close enough to the action to feel involved in, rather than distanced from the experience.

Despite the natural advantages provided by the design of the theatre, it must have required great skill, as well as a good script, to hold the attention of an audience for the two hours plus of the performance and to achieve the kind of effect on the groundlings so patronizingly dismissed by one of Shakespeare's contemporaries:

> On tiptoe to reach up,
> And (from rare silence) clap their brawny hands,
> T'applaud what their charmed soul scarce understands.
>
> (from the Prologue to Dekker's *If it be not good the devil is in it*, 1612)

The atmosphere in the theatre was lively and bustling, with people selling fruit and bottled beer. There was certainly no automatic and respectful hush of the kind that comes over a contemporary audience when the lights in the house dim and those on stage rise in intensity. Neither was there an audience already predisposed to like or appreciate a play simply because it had been written by Shakespeare. His name was certainly no better known than that of many contemporary dramatists, and it appears that audiences came to watch actors rather than specifically to see and hear the work of a particular dramatist. If there was a reputation to live up to, it almost certainly revolved around the name of the theatre company rather than that of any one individual. Their work was collective and collaborative, and the theatre itself was usually owned by a group of players (Shakespeare was a shareholder in the Globe). The 'great globe itself', and all the other theatres that mushroomed after Burbage built the first in 1576, were built as shops

75

designed to sell their theatrical products to consumers more effectively than the previous non-theatre-based arrangements had permitted. Their continued existence and prosperity entirely depended on the operation of the market, and their ability to create products desired by consumers. If they did not like what they saw, there was little reason for them to exercise the kind of embarrassed restraint and polite tolerance common in today's more inhibited theatre audiences. Both actors and audience shared the same space, were lit by the same light, and, despite the poetical and rhetorical heights scaled by Shakespeare, they basically spoke the same common language.

Apart from the theatrical activity of the south bank of the Thames, other parts of London contained so-called 'private theatres' also showing the plays of Shakespeare and other Elizabethan and Jacobean dramatists. The main difference between the public and private theatres, as far as we are concerned, was the scale of the auditorium and stage, and the social composition of the audience. Private theatres were constructed within existing buildings – probably the great halls of monastic buildings such as the Blackfriars theatre in London. Here, the auditorium was smaller than that of the public theatres and the audience faced the stage end-on. Plays were often performed at night with the audience and actors sharing the same source of illumination. It was more expensive to go to the private theatres and thus the audience was more likely to come from the educated and moneyed class. Although by the end of the first decade of the seventeenth century the private theatres were feeding an appetite for spectacle originating because of the hunger amongst aristocratic audiences for elaborate masques produced for the court (*The Tempest* is thought to have been first produced in a private theatre, and is certainly Shakespeare's most spectacular play, containing, as it does, a shipwreck, a banquet which mysteriously appears and disappears and a masque), the repertory of both public and private theatres was essentially interchangeable.

When attempting to animate a visual text for a play of this period, whether it was written for the public or private theatre is not really very significant. What is important to remember is the shape and size of the stage in relation to the auditorium; that entrances and exits were made through two doors; that there were three basic acting areas; and, perhaps most important of all, the performance convention governing both kinds of space was *non-representational*.

When you read Shakespeare you will not find in the printed texts a detailed plan as to how he wanted the action to be staged. Indeed, any dramatist, including Shakespeare, may not know the most effective way of actually staging an idea. But you can find evidence in the spoken text that will tell you, for example, the location of the action and help you to imagine what it might look like. Thus, the geographical location for the action of *Twelfth Night* is indicated, not by an elaborate architectural setting, but by the words spoken by the actors:

VIOLA
  What country, friends, is this?
CAPTAIN
  This is Illyria, Lady.
                (I, ii, lines 1–2)

Of course, this is not to suggest that the stage of the public or private theatre was clothed *only* by the imagination of the audience cued by the actors. It may well have been common practice to indicate a specific location, not only through language, but also by using a simply built stage construction, such as trees made out of canvas and wood that could be used to signify, say, the Forest of Arden. The balcony at the rear of the stage may have been used to represent the battlements of Flint Castle in *Richard II*, and the wall of the tiring-house itself may have had ladders placed against it in order to stage the scaling of the walls of Harfleur in Act Three, scene one of *Henry V*. But there was no attempt to imitate reality in terms of setting. Representational or illusionistic staging is a much later phenomenon that only really became possible in the mid nineteenth century. A 'tree' on the stage of the Globe during a performance of *As You Like It*, would be there to *represent* the reality of a forest, rather than attempting on any level to pretend to *be* a real tree in a real forest. The conventions of Shakespeare's theatre made no attempt to disguise the fact that the audiences were consuming, and the players manufacturing, fictions. The active collaboration of the audience's imagination was sometimes called upon to make up for the inability of the stage to create realistic images. As the chorus in *Henry V* says:

> . . . let us . . .
> *On your imaginary forces work.*
> *Suppose* within the girdle of these walls
> Are now confined two mighty monarchies,
> Whose high uprearèd and abutting fronts
> The perilous narrow ocean parts asunder.
> *Piece out our imperfections with your thoughts*:
> Into a thousand parts divide one man,
> And make *imaginary* puissance.
> *Think, when we talk of horses, that you see them*
> Printing their proud hoofs i' th' receiving earth;

> For *'tis your thoughts that now must deck our kings*,
> Carry them here and there, jumping o'er times,
> Turning th' accomplishment of many years
> Into an hour-glass . . .
> (Prologue, lines 17–31, author's italics)

But this seeming apology for the paucity of illusionistic resources can easily be misinterpreted to mean that Shakespeare would have automatically employed them had the technology been available to him. Where the action took place was obviously significant to Shakespeare as the exotic and diverse locations of his dramas reveal: Ancient Greece and Rome, Cyprus and Venice, Verona and Denmark, a tropical island. But, it is the *atmospheric* qualities of those locations, and the nature of the people who inhabit them, as revealed by what they say and do, that counts, not the physical attempt to realistically portray what the place might have looked like geographically or architecturally.

Creating elaborate and costly settings for Shakespeare's plays – settings frequently researched with reference to discoveries made by archaeologists – was a fashion that dominated nineteenth-century British productions of Shakespeare. They elevated the visual text to a position where it came to dominate, and even, at times, to entirely replace, the words spoken by actors. For instance, the attempt to re-create the illusion of a square in sixteenth-century Verona in a production of *Romeo and Juliet* had a terrific appeal to audiences. It was a delight and challenge to the eye in much the same way as spectacular cinematic presentations of disasters are now. But, not only did this approach mask the fact that, whatever the setting, Shakespeare was writing about England and the English, it also succeeded in creating illusionistic stage pictures that sacrificed meaning to spectacle. The Victorian theatre, especially, paid a price for using Shakespeare simply as a vehicle for scenic spectacle and illusion.

In order to look at what can happen to Shakespeare when the texts are reproduced within an illusionistic and spectacular convention I want to look at the opening scene of *The Tempest*, and at two performances of the play, which, although separated by more than 100 years, bear a remarkable resemblance to each other. The first played at the Princess Theatre in London in the summer of 1857, and was witnessed by, amongst others, Charles Dodgson, alias Lewis Carroll, the author of *Alice in Wonderland*. The second was seen by millions when John Gorrie's production was screened in 1979 as part of the BBC/Time Life Shakespeare series. Carroll recorded his visit to the theatre in his diary:

In the evening we visited the Princess's: the pieces were *A Game of Romps* [a one-act farce by J. B. Morton] and *The Tempest*. The scenic effects in *The Tempest* certainly surpass anything I ever saw there or elsewhere. The most marvellous was the ship-wreck in the first scene, where (to all appearance) a real ship is heaving on huge waves, and is finally wrecked under a cliff that reaches up to the roof. The machinery that works this must be something wonderful: the scene quite brought back to my mind the storm I saw at Whitby last year, and the vessels plunging through the harbour mouth.

(*Eyewitnesses of Shakespeare*, ed. Gamini Salgado, pp. 349–50)

But, as we have noted, such cinematic realism was not possible on the Elizabethan/Jacobean stage. However, realism, and the illusion of an actual shipwreck, was also apparently the desired effect of Gorrie's production for the BBC. Presumably, he wanted, like the stage manager of the Princess, to thrill a television audience with spectacle, for no apparent effort or expense was spared in using wind and wave machines, real water and the considerable electronic resources of the BBC's sound technicians, to simulate, for the viewer sitting comfortably in his or her living room, the experience of watching a ship sinking; but, *The Tempest* is *not* about the sinking of a ship. Unfortunately, the experience of watching either production probably resulted in, at best, a shared experience with the crew, rather than a shared understanding of the significance of the event itself.

Now, I want to look in detail at this short opening scene, and, as we did earlier with *Hamlet*, explore the clues given in the printed text as to how to re-create a visual text bearing in mind the conventions in use on the Jacobean stage. Do reread it before going on.

A tempestuous noise of thunder and lightning heard   I.1
Enter a Shipmaster and a Boatswain

MASTER
Boatswain!

BOATSWAIN
Here, Master. What cheer?

MASTER
Good. Speak to th'mariners. Fall to't, yarely, or we run ourselves aground. Bestir, bestir!   *Exit*
Enter Mariners

BOATSWAIN
Heigh, my hearts! Cheerly, cheerly, my hearts! Yare, yare! Take in the topsail! Tend to th'Master's whistle! – Blow till thou burst thy wind, if room enough.

Enter Alonso, Sebastian, Antonio, Ferdinand, Gonzalo, and others

ALONSO
Good Boatswain, have care. Where's the Master? Play the men.

BOATSWAIN

I pray now, keep below.

ANTONIO

Where is the Master, Boatswain?

BOATSWAIN

Do you not hear him? You mar our labour. Keep your cabins! You do assist the storm.

GONZALO

Nay, good, be patient.

BOATSWAIN

When the sea is. Hence! What cares these roarers for the name of king? To cabin! Silence! Trouble us not.

GONZALO

Good, yet remember whom thou hast aboard.

BOATSWAIN

None that I more love than myself. You are a councillor. If you can command these elements to silence, and work the peace of the present, we will not hand a rope more. Use your authority. If you cannot, give thanks you have lived so long, and make yourself ready in your cabin for the mischance of the hour, if it so hap. – Cheerly, good hearts! – Out of our way, I say!

Exit

GONZALO

I have great comfort from this fellow. Methinks he hath no drowning-mark upon him: his complexion is perfect gallows. Stand fast, good Fate, to his hanging. Make the rope of his destiny our cable, for our own doth little advantage. If he be not born to be hanged, our case is miserable.

Exeunt Gonzalo and the other nobles

Enter Boatswain

BOATSWAIN

Down with the topmast! Yare! Lower, lower! Bring her to try with main-course.

A cry within

A plague upon this howling! They are louder than the weather, or our office.

Enter Sebastian, Antonio, and Gonzalo

Yet again? What do you here? Shall we give o'er and drown? Have you a mind to sink?

SEBASTIAN

A pox o'your throat, you bawling, blasphemous, incharitable dog!

BOATSWAIN

Work you, then.

ANTONIO

Hang, cur, hang, you whoreson, insolent noise-maker! We are less afraid to be drowned than thou art.

GONZALO

I'll warrant him for drowning, though the ship were no stronger than a nutshell and as leaky as an unstanched wench.

BOATSWAIN

Lay her a-hold, a-hold! Set her two courses! Off to sea again! Lay her off!

Enter Mariners wet

MARINERS

All lost! To prayers, to prayers! All lost!   *Exeunt*

BOATSWAIN

What, must our mouths be cold?

GONZALO

The King and Prince at prayers, let's assist them,

For our case is as theirs.

SEBASTIAN   I'm out of patience.

ANTONIO

We are merely cheated of our lives by drunkards.

This wide-chopped rascal – would thou mightst lie drowning

The washing of ten tides!

GONZALO   He'll be hanged yet,

Though every drop of water swear against it,

And gape at wid'st to glut him.

A confused noise within: 'Mercy on us!' – 'We split, we split!' – 'Farewell,
my wife and children!' – 'Farewell, brother!' – 'We split, we split, we split!'

Exit Boatswain

ANTONIO

Let's all sink wi'th'King.

SEBASTIAN

Let's take leave of him.   *Exit, with Antonio*

GONZALO

Now would I give a thousand furlongs of sea for an acre of barren ground.
Long heath, brown furze, anything. The wills above be done, but I would fain
die a dry death.   *Exit*

The opening directions state:

[On a ship at sea]: *A tempestuous noise of thunder and lightning heard*

This indicates that all the considerable energy and resources of the
Jacobean stage-crew would have been called upon to make the sounds
of a storm at sea. Unlike the BBC, they could not use the recorded
sound of a real storm, they had to find ways of making sounds that
would serve to *represent* that storm. Unlike their descendants at the
Princess Theatre, they would have had no elaborate hydraulic machinery to simulate the moving ship, and, on entering the stage, the
players enacting the Master and the Boatswain would have used their
physical skills to imitate the movement of men trying to keep their balance
on the slippery deck of a moving vessel. Costumes would have provided
the audience with information about their characters' calling and status.

These impressions, established through the visual text, are then confirmed by the spoken – an exchange of titles reveals who the two actors represent:

MASTER
  Boatswain!
BOATSWAIN
  Here, Master.

The Master is the first to speak. He alerts his second-in-command (and the audience) to the imminent danger that faces them, and gives the orders to 'Speak to th'mariners'. Thus, the opening minutes of the action establish the storm (through simple sound effects); that what is happening takes place on board a ship (through the physical gestures of the actors and the spoken reference to 'th'mariners'); the status of those being represented (through their costumes and any gestures, such as a salute, that might indicate the ship's hierarchy) and the circumstances that now threaten the lives of the men on board: 'we run ourselves aground'. As the Master exits he apparently relinquishes command: he has given orders but left the execution of them to the Boatswain, who is now in charge of the efforts to save the ship, its passengers and crew.

The crew now enters; the greeting of the Boatswain, 'Heigh, my hearts! Cheerly, cheerly, my hearts!', perhaps indicates that the first task of this group of actors is to signal to the audience their understandable unease and misgiving. The Boatswain encourages them with his warm greeting; his knowledge of what to do in order to combat the threat to the good order and safety of the ship is reassuring. There is no uncertainty here; his orders are clear. What the audience should see is not a minor technological miracle: the mirage of a real storm and ship at sea, but, instead, they should be made to focus on the men's ordered and purposeful response to the threat of chaos. Everyone on the ship now knows what to do, and when and how to do it. The audience need to be given time to register this before the arrival of the second group of actors, those representing the court of King Alonso of Naples.

This second group is in marked visual contrast to the first. The sailors' costumes may have been simple – possibly ragged and with bare feet – but those worn by the King and his court would immediately signal, not only their vastly superior wealth and status, but also their total inappropriateness for a ship at sea in a storm. But, the telling contrast comes because, unlike the mariners, *they do not know what to do.* They have no access to skills, nor any knowledge or experience that will equip them to respond to the crisis. They are out of their element.

The actor playing the character with the highest rank speaks first. As befits a king, Alonso assumes that he is, or should be, in command. He issues two orders and asks a question:

> Good Boatswain, have care. Where's the Master?
> Play the men. (I, i, 9–10)

Alonso's first instinct is to give an order; his second to seek the highest available authority. He obviously finds it difficult to accept that the Boatswain is in charge of the ship, and, therefore, also in charge of him. Instead of getting the immediate answer his rank and position could reasonably lead him to expect, he and the rest of his company are brushed aside by the Boatswain, who issues a blunt instruction of his own: 'keep below'. Of course, this is meant literally, but in the context of the scene it can also mean 'keep below me', that is, accept that it is *I*, a humble Boatswain, and not *you*, a powerful king, who is in command here. This constitutes a total inversion of the strict social hierarchy of Elizabethan and Jacobean England. One of the King's company (Antonio) won't accept this brusque command from a social inferior, and steps forward to confront the Boatswain. In doing so he is acting on behalf of the King without waiting for permission, thus challenging, not only the authority of the Boatswain, but also that of the King. He repeats the King's question. The Boatswain's response is sharp and angry:

> Do you not hear him? [the Master] You mar our labour.
> Keep your cabins! You do assist the storm.
>
> (I, i, 13–14)

It indicates, in the din and bustle still presumably being kept up on stage, but *not* being allowed to divert attention away from the actors who are speaking, that the voice of the Master can be heard issuing commands to other groups of mariners. But the Boatswain does what the Jacobean audience would have recognized as unthinkable, even treasonable, on dry land: he *orders* the King's party to 'keep your cabins'. There is no immediate indication that they intend to comply. Thus, the conflict of the elements is mirrored in this, the first of many conflicts of authority chronicled in this play.

It is the 'honest old councillor', Gonzalo, who, perhaps literally, steps between Antonio and the Boatswain. He tries to calm the situation by reminding the Boatswain of his social obligations: 'remember whom thou hast aboard.' But the Boatswain is concerned with a far more fundamental issue than the observance of social conventions: he is trying to preserve the lives of all on board. He has to remind Gonzalo (and the King) of an important truth:

If you can command these elements to silence, and work the peace of the present, we will not hand a rope more. Use your authority. If you cannot, give thanks you have lived so long . . . (I, i, 21–4)

The authority of a king is not absolute. On this ship, threatened as it is with extinction, it is of no consequence; here, power and control are vested in the Boatswain and the crew. Other men, however exalted their rank, live their day-to-day lives in a very different environment to this, and are now simply in the way. Authority is vested in a boatswain, not a king. Gonzalo's wisdom as a councillor now asserts itself. He appears to recognize that compromise is necessary and acquiesces with the commands of his social inferior. He sees that, rough though his manner may be, his logic is faultless: 'I have great comfort from this fellow.'

Whilst the Boatswain and the aristocrats have been in contention as to whose authority carries the more weight, the crew have not been talking, but have been working. The Boatswain, when he re-enters, reaffirms his authority. He is sure and precise (and here Shakespeare, as many subsequent editors of this play have pointed out, was at pains to be accurate) in the orders he now issues to the crew:

Down with the topmast! Yare! Lower, lower! Bring her to try with main-course. (I, i, 34–5)

But, no sooner is he seen to be controlling and managing the crew's expert response to this threat to all the lives of those on board, than his authority is again challenged. The re-entry of Sebastian, Antonio and Gonzalo signals a renewed human conflict. Unlike the King and the Prince, who had the wisdom to listen to good counsel and retire below, surrendering their authority (to that of the Boatswain and, ultimately, to that of God, to whom they now pray), Antonio and Sebastian will not accept that anyone other than themselves should exercise control of their destinies. The point being made here is that whoever commands the ship (or the ship of state, which the vessel metaphorically represents) governs, effectively, *only* with the consent of all those on board; Antonio and Sebastian withhold their consent. Their subsequent confrontation with the Boatswain degenerates into an exchange of insults. A verbal storm erupts which, in its ferocity, almost matches that of the tempest itself:

BOATSWAIN

Yet again? What do you here? Shall we give o'er and drown? Have you a mind to sink?

SEBASTIAN

A pox o'your throat, you bawling, blasphemous, incharitable dog!

BOATSWAIN

Work you, then.

ANTONIO

Hang, cur, hang, you whoreson, insolent noise-maker! We are less afraid to be drowned than thou art. (I, i, 38–44)

The famous stage direction, *Enter Mariners wet*, signals the end of the confrontation and the beginning of the end of the scene. Until this point is reached, the ship's crew are seen to be coping with the tempest; but, after this fierce argument, there is a demonstrable sign (the wet mariners) that things are taking a turn for the worse. The men have apparently given up hope that their own efforts can save them, and, like King Alonso, they, too, resort to prayer. Gonzalo tries unsuccessfully to counsel Antonio and Sebastian to join them, but, prayer does not appeal (they won't accept God's authority either). Against all the evidence they try to blame the Boatswain and his crew for their present predicament:

> We are merely cheated of our lives by drunkards.
> This wide-chopped rascal – would thou mightst lie
>   drowning
> The washing of ten tides! (I, i, 64–7)

The climax of the scene comes with the breaking up of the ship. The printed text seems to imply the use of improvisation in performance, both on the part of the actors and the stage-crew. The latter are now required, not only to create the sound of a storm, but also a '*confused noise within*'. As so often happens in Shakespeare, the more extreme the situation, the more simple and direct the language used to express it: 'Mercy on us!', 'Farewell, my wife and children!', 'Farewell, brother!'. These cries may well move an audience to experience compassion. The concluding lines are given to Gonzalo. Despite his understandable desire to be anywhere other than where he now finds himself, he is nevertheless resigned to the will of a superior authority: 'The wills above be done.'

In most performances of *The Tempest* that I have seen, this opening scene is driven along at a gale-force pace. But, despite the amount of activity that is going on, it is necessary to resist the temptation to surrender the performance to the demands of spectacle. If the audience aren't able to reflect on the *significance* of what is happening because they are too caught up with the vicarious experience of men in danger, then Shakespeare's careful exposition of the *ideas* to be subsequently negotiated in the play will fail. Shakespeare's theatre could not realistically attempt to illustrate a ship at sea in a storm; indeed, he almost seems to anticipate Brecht in his decision not to give names to the characters, but, instead, to lay stress on their social roles rather than on their personalities. The Victorian theatre could, if Lewis Carroll is to be believed, re-create a spectacular storm-toss'd bark, and the BBC certainly didn't lack the resources required for verisimilitude, but, it is *not* the storm that matters; what is important is that we see how different individuals react to it. It is a test in which some do well, others badly. The critical situation (engineered by Prospero) affords an opportunity for the audience to witness, not how like this storm is to a real storm, witnessed at Whitby or wherever, but to recognize the wisdom of Gonzalo, the modesty of the King and Prince, their understanding of the nature of their authority and the naked and irrational aggression of Sebastian and Antonio. The visual images built into this text, and arising logically from it, are designed to act as metaphors carrying responsibility for meaning and are not there simply to provide a theatre with an excuse for creating vicarious thrills.

Costume

In reading Shakespeare it is important to pay attention to any direct or indirect reference to what characters are wearing, for, in performance, costume generates a whole series of signs and signals that are 'read' by audiences. Similarly, in our day-to-day lives, clothes, and the way in which they are worn, are highly significant. They are part of the way in which consciously or unconsciously we express our personality and status. To some extent, what we wear will produce, at least initially, both positive and negative reactions in those we meet. Clothes are used, not only to make individual statements, but also to signal membership of particular groups in society ... young people's clothes are usually very different from those of old people. Clothes are also worn to signal a particular role in society; members of the clergy and emergency services wear distinctive uniforms, for example.

Costumes worn by actors are often used to locate the action on stage both historically and geographically. They can be used, as we saw in our analysis of Act One, scene one of *The Tempest*, to highlight divisions in social class or status, and can signify outwardly an inner change in the character wearing them, as happens in *King Lear*. Lear's mental disintegration is mirrored by his progression from regal garments to near nakedness. Of course, costumes can also create splendid visual images and, when required, can be used to create a special focus on one individual. Costumes can be used in more technical ways to create a focus of attention, for example, in a production of Shakespeare's *Henry VIII* at Stratford in 1983, the designer, Deirdrie Clancy, used colour in her costumes in key areas (on caps, bodices, cuffs) in order to concentrate attention on the eyes, faces and hands of the cast. Not least, costume is vitally important for the performer who has to wear it, as Sinead Cusack revealed when discussing her role of Katherine in Michael Bogdanov's production of *The Taming of the Shrew* for the RSC in 1978:

I knew it was radically wrong. It was exquisite, but I told Bob Crowley, the designer, that Kate wouldn't wear this dress. Her father might have bought it for her, but she wouldn't please him by wearing it. So I said, 'Let's desecrate it.' I wore boots underneath it. Bob came up to my dressing room, and we had this gorgeous pink silk dress hanging there, and he said, 'Shall I make the first cut?' He took a pair of scissors and he slashed the skirt, then I slashed the skirt. Then it felt right. It was as if Kate had said, 'Sure, I'll wear your dress – just look at it!'
(*Clamorous Voices*, p. xxiii)

Like Ms Cusack, an audience watching Shakespeare in the sixteenth or seventeenth century would have been very aware of the significance of what people wore. They experienced an elaborate contemporary dress code which was actually enshrined in law (although the extent to which the dress code was enforced is uncertain). We do know that certain kinds of material were, nominally at least, reserved for particular social groups. In any case, materials like velvet and brocade would have been excluded by cost from the wardrobes of all but the very wealthy. In Britain and America today it is much more difficult to tell the difference between social groups simply on the basis of their clothes, but there are recognizable broad categories of dress codes that distinguish young, urban, working-class black youths from, say, Sloane Rangers or Daughters of the American Revolution. The Elizabethan dress code was elaborate and complex, and extended to the use of particular colours as well as to the way in which clothes were worn. Despite this, the signs that they emitted could be as readily decoded on the stage as on the street.

In the Elizabethan theatre, costumes were certainly a vital ingredient in making successful performances of Shakespeare. They were also, for the Elizabethan actor, his most valued and valuable possession. Costumes worn by actors were sometimes bequeathed or purchased from the nobility. Such clothes were fabulously expensive and tailored from fine materials normally unavailable to most people, even if they could afford to buy them. The inventory of one of the Elizabethan players' companies (Henslowe's) gives a vivid description of the kind of garments that were to be seen on the Elizabethan stage:

1 A scarlett cloke wth brode gould Laces: w^{t} gould buttons of the sam downe the sids
2 ... A scarlett cloke Layd downe w^{t} silver Lace and silver buttens ...

(Michael Hattaway, *Elizabethan Popular Theatre*, p. 86)

The costumes were worn without very much regard to either period or historical accuracy; leading players had their own from which they selected as they saw fit. The company wardrobe was also used by the hired men and contained, according to Michael Hattaway, costumes that could be 'read' by audiences in the following ways:

characters of high degree wore robes with heraldic or ecclesiastical emblems ... doctors' gowns were of scarlet, lawyers' gowns of black, rustics and clowns wore 'startups' (boots that reached to mid-calf), allowed fools wore long coats of motley woven of coarse wool and part coloured green and yellow ... virgins wore white, prologues wore black ... shepherds wore white coats and carried staff and bottle, sailors wore canvas suits, servants bluecoats or slops.

(Ibid., p. 87)

A stage bedecked with kings and queens, lords and ladies, the great, if not the good, must, indeed, have been a spectacular sight, if only for the contrast between the clothes worn by most of the audience and those sported by the actors. The wearing of clothes technically belonging to the aristocracy was not unproblematic. Actors were men of humble origins. Clothed as they were, they seemed to some (especially to the Puritans with their rigid ideas about degree) to lay claim to a status to which they had no legitimate claim. In *Tudor Drama and Politics*, David Bevington shows how this tension between the players and the power they imitated was effectively used to make political observations. No wonder the Puritans so vehemently objected to the players who, as far as they were concerned, not only flouted the rules of conduct that sustained the social order, but also did so with apparent impunity and before others who might choose to follow their example:

In Stage Plays for a boy to put on the attyre, the gesture, the passions of a woman; for a meane person to take upon the title of a Prince with counterfeit porte, and traine, is by outward signs to show themselves otherwise than they are, and so within the compasse of a lye ... We are commanded by God to abide in the same calling wherein we were called, which is our ordinary vocation in a commonweale ... If privat men be suffered to forsake theire calling because they desire to walke gentlemen-like in sattine and velvet, with a bucler at their heeles, proportion is so broken, unitie dissolved, harmony confounded, that the whole body must be dismembered and the prince or the head cannot chuse but sicken.   (Stephen Gosson, *Plays Confuted in Five Actions*, London, 1582)

But costume on the Elizabethan stage was not simply worn to amaze and astonish the groundlings, or to deliberately antagonize the Puritans. It could be used in a very sophisticated way as part of the visual text. In *Action is Eloquence*, Bevington cites the following example of how costume can be used to make meaning:

King Lear's journey from regal autocracy through madness to tearful reconciliation with Cordelia is signalled at every crucial turning by what he wears, by his royal robes, by his running 'unbonneted' in the storm, by the 'lendings' at which he tears and the weeds with which he is madly bedecked, by the 'fresh garments' suited to his royal rank in which he is vested at Cordelia's behest.   (*Action is Eloquence*, p. 2)

Perhaps the best, and certainly the best-known, example of the potential of costume to make eloquent statements in performance is provided by Hamlet. Shakespeare is careful and deliberate when he specifies his hero's 'inky cloak' and 'customary suits of solemn black' (I, ii, lines 77–8). Of course, while this costume serves as an outward display of Hamlet's state of mourning for the death of his father and of his rebellion against the recent remarriage of his mother, it could also serve, as far as an Elizabethan audience were concerned, to link Hamlet's condition with melancholia, a fashionable state much affected by young men of rank. But the costume also acts emblematically: it prefigures death. Throughout the play Hamlet's costume continually links him to death: from mourning that of his father, to causing that of Polonius, Claudius and Laertes, and being in part responsible for the deaths of his mother and Ophelia. He is also appropriately dressed for his own funeral.

On a practical rather than a symbolic level, Hamlet's costume isolates him visually from all the other characters with whom he appears on-stage; it works like a spotlight in drawing the attention of the audience to him. This simple, but effective, device is seen to work to good effect from the first time that the audience see Hamlet. In the first scene of the play, the audience have seen the Ghost of Hamlet's father and know, before the Prince himself, that something is indeed 'rotten in the state of Denmark' (I, iv, line 90). But, what is wrong, and why, remains as much of a mystery to them as to Horatio and the other on-stage witnesses of the extraordinary events in that famous opening scene. What the audience *do* know is that the apparition, dumb to Horatio, *will* speak to Hamlet. His name is presented to the audience at the end of the first scene as belonging to the character who will be the key to the answers of the questions posed; Hamlet is the detective who, the audience hope and expect, will unravel the clues to their satisfaction. At the beginning of scene two, his appearance immediately enables the audience to put a face (and a costume) to the name they already know and from whom they expect so much.

Hamlet's entry on to the stage is accordingly carefully prepared by Shakespeare. Scene two opens with a procession on to the stage. It is a formal entrance of a large group of players representing characters being seen by the audience for the first time. In the procession are Claudius, Gertrude, Polonius, Laertes, Voltemand, Cornelius, Councillors, Attendants and Hamlet. The entrance heralds a state occasion, and one that, in this case, begins with important and pressing political business. The audience see Claudius exercising his recently acquired power. The status of both he, and his Queen, Gertrude, needs to be immediately recognized by the audience. Costume would, of course, be an obvious way of signalling this. In theory, the action should be dominated by Claudius; he is, after all, not only the most senior person present, but also enacts his kingly role with considerable assurance, giving orders for the direction of the affairs of state with calm authority. What Claudius has to *say* does monopolize the page (he speaks virtually the whole of the opening forty-nine lines), but on the stage his words are heard in a context that includes the brooding, silent, but highly visible figure in the 'inky cloak', Hamlet. Because of this visual counterpoint to what would otherwise be a scene dominated by Claudius, it is not surprising that the first lines that Hamlet speaks are not delivered to any character on-stage, but are addressed to the audience in the theatre. In a sense, in performance, theirs is a special relationship in which they receive privileged information. In the first scene, Shakespeare has written a performance text in which he does everything he can to ensure that the audience have heightened expectations of the Prince of Denmark. Now, his black costume signals a Prince who, far from being at the centre of life at Court, is out of place and marginal. It also ensures that the audience never take their eyes off him.

As we have seen, in plays by Shakespeare (and his contemporaries), clothes worn by actors on-stage in performance were never simply a means of self-advertisement and display. They could be used (as in *King Lear*) to express the changing inner state of a character's mind, and costume in *Hamlet* is seen to tell the audience something about, not only the character's state of mind, but also his relationship to those around him and to alert the audience to the tragic nature of the events to come.

In *Macbeth* there is an even more powerful and interesting use of costume at work in constructing meanings in the text in performance. In Act Three, scene four, a banquet has been prepared for Macbeth. The meal is an important public and state occasion for the new King and his Queen. It is an opportunity for both to display and enjoy in public the outward signs of power and privilege that the bloody coup has recently brought them. To do this they employ, I suggest, the conventional signs of royal status: rich clothes, jewels and, perhaps, emblems of state such as a crown and coronet. Lady Macbeth acts as the hostess at what ought to be, for both her and her husband, a triumphal affirmation of all that they have done. It is, I think, particularly important to consider what Lady Macbeth wears at this, her first state banquet as queen. Her costume should be chosen to emphasize her new social and political status, and the corresponding gain in both material wealth and power. As we know, the banquet is not a triumph, but a disaster for Macbeth and his wife; the elaborate display of hospitality, the sharing of a meal, and the attempt by Macbeth to reaffirm the stability of the new social order, 'You know your own degrees, sit down. At first/And last the hearty welcome' (III, iv, lines 1–2), is fatally undermined by the appearance to Macbeth of Banquo's ghost. The outward display of regal behaviour is fractured and the public mask of Macbeth is stripped away to reveal his private terror. The effectiveness of this in performance can be helped if Macbeth's costume, like that of his wife, is one that emphasizes his temporal power and the dignity of his office. Robes that signify the possession of high and dignified office are thus made to appear truly ill-fitting and inappropriate by Banquo's appearance. Macbeth must appear, by the end of the scene, to be what he is, a man impersonating a legitimate king.

If Lady Macbeth has also been shown in this scene in the costume of a powerful queen, intent on impressing others with the legitimacy of her new status, then the shock to the audience of the contrast between that image and what is seen on the next occasion when Lady Macbeth enters the stage alone, will be so much greater. Then, in Act Five, scene one, the famous sleepwalking scene, she appears, literally, stripped of the outward signs, symbols and show of personal and political power for which she was prepared to risk anything and sacrifice anybody. Now the audience see her, not as a public figure, but as a private individual. Thus, radical change is signalled by her new costume: Shakespeare is careful to specify that she is to appear in her nightgown.

After the murder of Duncan, those characters who are awakened are also, presumably, seen to enter the stage in their nightgowns, for they are subsequently told to 'put on manly readiness' (II, iii, line 130). We can assume the murdered king was killed in his nightgown. As Alan Dessen has pointed out, 'the associations with interrupted sleep or other disturbances at night sometimes link nightgowns or unready dress with troubled consciences' (*Elizabethan Stage Conventions and Modern Interpreters*, p. 18). Hence, through the costume, a visual link is established between the appearance of Lady Macbeth and the responsibility for regicide. The actual costume worn by the performer is not necessarily a flimsy piece of material barely concealing the body. But it is a significant direction by Shakespeare because it is a garment worn in the privacy of the bedchamber, simple and relatively unadorned, and certainly not, unlike her previous clothes, designed for public display. Yet this scene *is* public; Lady Macbeth appears under the watchful eyes of those two minor, but in this scene significant, characters: the Doctor and the Gentlewoman. Their presence, and Lady Macbeth's appearance in her nightgown, is Shakespeare's way of making clear to the audience her new and highly vulnerable status. She is exposed to the gaze of others as she attempts to scrutinize herself. The nightgown symbolizes the stripping away of the public outer shell, and what lies underneath is a woman alone and helpless. Shakespeare has literally and symbolically stripped her of her power, subdued her, and made her appear weak, something he never does with Macbeth whose masculine image is left intact, and who dies fighting. The change in Lady Macbeth from a confident, powerful and, to the Elizabethan male mind, deeply threatening figure, to a pitiful and vulnerable woman, registers on the collective consciousness of the audience because, in part, that change is signalled in the visual text through costume.

Before leaving the subject of costume, it should be noted that it is not always necessary to imagine its use in the way I have just outlined. For example, Trevor Nunn's 1976 production of *Macbeth* for the RSC (designed by John Napier) opened up an interesting range of possible interpretations through the use of costume. Each player, from Ian McKellen (Macbeth) to Judi Dench (Lady Macbeth), wore whatever seemed to the designer and director appropriate for his or her character *regardless* of historical accuracy or period consistency. The point being established was that *Macbeth* is not about events that took place a long time ago, when people believed in witchcraft and ghosts, and is therefore distanced from us, but, that it is a play about the power of evil – and evil is timeless.

In the previous chapter on the performer's text, I suggested that our current theatre practice in staging Shakespeare is dominated by the influence of the director. There are some who now argue that the designer has begun to challenge the director for supremacy in the creative process. Paola Dionisotti, an actress who has worked a lot with the RSC, certainly feels that there is a:

consensus of thought . . . that you have to fill that space [the stage of the main house at Stratford, and the Barbican stage in London] with very powerful images all the time or you'll lose the audience . . . many directors seem to have very little visual sense, so they are utterly dependent upon their designers, designers who, it turns out, are directing the directors, telling them, 'You've got to create this picture with the performance at this point.' The images become what the play is 'about'. In the 1960s critics talked about 'director's theatre'; in the 1980s, about 'designer's theatre'. (*Clamorous Voices*, p. xxi)

Not surprisingly for an actress, Ms Dionisotti defends the primacy of language: 'Theatre began with the word.' Perhaps the 1990s and beyond will signal a renaissance of the power of the actor and of the words he or she speaks in performance. Certainly, the meteoric rise to prominence of a company founded by an actor, and one which performs a good deal of Shakespeare (Kenneth Branagh's Renaissance Theatre), seems to indicate that directors and designers will not have things all their own way in the 1990s. But whoever contests the control over the process of reproducing Shakespeare, the active reader of his plays must always acknowledge that the nature of theatre is that words, however beautiful or poetic, are only understood in a given context, and supplying that context is a vital part of the business of making meanings. I hope this chapter on the visual text will remind you of how important it is, when you are reading a play, to *look* critically at the concrete images that form in your imagination, as well as listening to what is being said.

Theatrical Ephemera?

Stage Properties

Many now highly distinguished actors have begun their careers as spear-carriers in productions of classic plays in the British repertoire. It is lowly but dignified work, and, as we have seen, not without the potential for creating meanings in the text in performance. With or without a spear, the silent actor is always signifying something to an audience whenever he or she is on-stage. But I want, in this chapter, to focus not so much on the actor, but on the spear.

In Ron Daniel's production of *Hamlet* for the RSC, which opened at Stratford in the late summer of 1984, a total of fifty-three properties were required. They ranged from the obvious – a vial of poison (for use in the dumb show 'killing' of old Hamlet, III, ii), 'five or six skulls' and a quantity of bones (required by the grave diggers in V, i), and a poison ring (needed by Claudius in V, v) – to the obscure – a make-up box (for the players in III, ii) and a handkerchief ('white with a black border') for Hamlet's use throughout the play. Such a large number of props is by no means unusual, some are required by the text (one of the skulls presumably has to belong to Yorick), and others, such as the handkerchief, are included because the director or the actor feels that their use will help his or her performance.

Important as they may be in performance, stage properties, particularly small so-called personal props carried or worn by individual actors (such as fans, rings, books, etc.), are usually ignored by even the most attentive readers. They can, however, play a significant role in the way in which meanings are constructed and transmitted. The diaries of Sir Peter Hall, lately director of the Royal National Theatre, provide a mine, not just of good gossip, but also some fascinating material about the process of text-into-performance in the contemporary theatre. At one point Hall gives a first-hand account of the effect of properties on actors in rehearsal:

We rehearsed the *Hamlet* graveyard scene this morning with a real skull. The actuality of the scene was immediately apparent; actors, stage management, everybody aware of a dead man's skull among us ...

(*Peter Hall's Diaries*, p. 189)

Properties then, may inspire and stimulate the work of a group of players. They also can, as Hall's notes reveal, point to practical problems of staging of which the play reader is often totally unaware. Of that same scene, Hall identifies a series of problems:

Where can you keep the spade? Where can you put the coffin? How does Laertes get in and out? [of Ophelia's grave] How do the gravediggers get in and out?

(Ibid., p. 194)

When the practicalities have been satisfactorily resolved, the focus can turn to the interpretative significance of properties in the performance text. Properties can help in the creation of a particular mood and atmosphere, they can establish, together with the setting and costumes, the historical period in which the action is set, and their use by a particular character can lend positive or negative associations to that individual. A particular choice of property to be used by an actor can impose, or at least reinforce, a particular directorial interpretation of a scene. For example, in Act Two, scene four of Nicholas Hytner's RSC production of *King Lear* in 1990, the text of Lear, Goneril and Regan stresses the age of the King: 'O, Sir! you are old'. Throughout the scene the audience listens to the discourse aware that, in the background, the director has placed a silent figure (suggesting a nurse) standing beside a wheelchair, holding a thick rug ready to drape it over the knees of the prospective invalid (Lear). It was a chilling sight, and, when the chair was moved forward by Goneril (Estelle Kohler) on 'I pray you, father, being weak, *seem* so', Lear (John Wood) up-ended it and cried out 'I prithee, daughter, do not *make* me mad'.

It is helpful to make a distinction – as they do in the theatre – between movable stage properties, such as beds, chairs, benches, candlesticks, vases of flowers and so on, and personal props. Both categories have their uses in staging Shakespeare. The Elizabethan/Jacobean theatre made extensive use of them, and relied on audiences being able to 'read' their correct association. For example:

Beds in Shakespeare are ... apt to juxtapose innocence with intrusion and violation. The bed's traditional associations of peace and intimacy are invoked as a backdrop to violence and death [the murder of Desdemona by Othello actually on their marriage-bed is a classic example of this] much as the throne serves to put spectators in mind of a majesty that is often desecrated. [The use of the throne is particularly significant in *Richard II*.]   (*Action is Eloquence*, p. 129)

The inventive and *appropriate* use of personal properties in performance was admired by the actor Ian McKellen in the Channel 4 series *Playing Shakespeare* (screened in 1984, with a book, based on the series, by John Barton, published by Methuen in the same year). In discussion with John Barton, he referred to the Peter Hall production of *Hamlet* to which we have already given some attention. The actor's eye noted that:

Claudius always had a glass with a drink in it, and because it was tumbler-shaped I knew that the liquid in it was whisky. That told me something precise about Claudius: he drinks whisky. It wasn't your all-purpose goblet with nothing in it but watered-down blackcurrant juice ... In the same production Polonius carried a briefcase and that was also relevant in a good way. You know what's in a briefcase; there are papers – to do with law and politics. It wasn't some sort of mocked-up Elizabethan satchel or a scroll which you couldn't believe had anything written on it!   (*Playing Shakespeare*, p. 181)

When Shakespeare specifies the use of a property as part of the action (as he does, for example, in Act Five, scene one of *Macbeth*, where Lady Macbeth is sleepwalking carrying a lighted taper), he often intends it to work as a visual metaphor as well as being an important element in establishing an appropriate mood and atmosphere. The lighted taper carried by Lady Macbeth in the sleepwalking scene functions on several different levels. It signalled to the original audience watching the play in daylight, in the open-air, that the action was taking place at night, but it also worked symbolically, representing a highly vulnerable and small light of conscience in an otherwise dark and lost soul.

A property can be used in a specific way by an actor to enhance the theatricality of a scene by drawing attention to some aspect of it. For example, in Trevor Nunn's 1976 RSC production of *Macbeth* (which had Judi Dench as Lady Macbeth), at one point in the sleep-walking scene she knelt down behind a block of wood on which was placed a lighted candle. She put her hands on either side of the flame as if to scrutinize them more closely for the blood of Duncan. The action vividly focused the attention of the audience on her murderous hands.

The prop in this scene from *Macbeth* could be used for something else too. It is important, I think, that the audience, and perhaps the performer, should sense that the flame could actually be extinguished. The resulting recognition of the risk being taken in performance by the actress is imparted to the audience and both reflects and intensifies their concern for her plight. In other words, the taper signifies, in this dramatic context, a series of connected ideas about the forces of light and dark at war in the play. It can also be used theatrically to make an audience *feel* the threat to order (the order under threat being the smooth running of the performance) that is experienced if it is thought that the flame might go out.

The creative use of properties in performance to make atmosphere through establishing a sense of risk is nowhere better illustrated than in Peter Brook's, now almost legendary, production of *A Midsummer Night's Dream* for the RSC in 1970. Brook has subsequently said that he saw his real theatrical challenge in staging this play to a contemporary audience, was getting them to experience, if not to believe in, the magical world in which the action takes place. His task was to discover, together with his actors, a theatre-language that was capable of articulating that magical world. The skilful use of properties formed part of the vocabulary of magic. In Act Two, scene one, Puck is instructed by Oberon to locate a charm:

> Fetch me that flower – the herb that I showed thee once.
> The juice of it on sleeping eyelids laid
> Will make or man or woman madly dote
> Upon the next live creature that it sees.

> (lines 169–72)

In the performance, Puck re-entered after his magical journey on a trapeze. He held the magic charm (represented by a spinning, silver disc), balanced on the end of a long flexible rod. On seeing him, Oberon, also swinging gently on a trapeze but at a lower level, looked up to ask, 'Hast thou the flower there? Welcome, wanderer' (line 247). As the Fairy King spoke these lines, Puck leant over and flipped the disc down so that it fell. Instead of hitting the ground it was caught by Oberon, also using a long rod with which he continued the disc's momentum. In the split second that it took for the disc to fall and be caught, a surge of excitement ran through the audience, touching and uniting them in a shared 'magical' moment. It was an old circus trick that worked through a combination of imagination, courage and skill on the part of the actors; it worked for the spectators because they knew the feat was not foolproof: the trick *could* fail, the magic was that it didn't.

In the example I have just given, a director used his imagination to augment Shakespeare's text. By using a property – a spinning disc – Brook's actors made magic appear concrete, real, and, above all, possible on the stage. The audience could apprehend what their conscious minds would probably never comprehend: the magical world of the play. Brook's grasp of theatricality unlocked a response to the text that a rational/scientific culture has largely precluded.

Some of the most effective use of props that I have seen was in Terry Hands's production of *Richard II* for the RSC. We have already discussed this production in terms of the casting of Richard and Bolingbroke; now I want to look at how properties were used by the director and actors in order to emphasize the differences between the two characters. Alan Howard played Richard as a man thoroughly at home with the ritual and ceremonial life of the court. He was supremely good at enacting the role of the king, his body and voice aptly constructed 'To monarchize, be feared, and kill with looks'. David Suchet's Bolingbroke, on the other hand, was a man ill at ease with the public obligations of kingship, much more a behind-the-scenes politician than a figurehead. In the deposition scene (IV, i), the director emphasized the importance of the regalia – the orb, sceptre and crown – that are crucial elements in the meaning of the scene. The crown is, of course, the symbol of kingship and power. Worn by the monarch on all major public and state occasions, it immediately signalled the status of the wearer as unique amongst men. The sceptre is the symbol of personal sovereignty, and the orb (a sphere with a cross attached) symbolizes the universal sovereignty of the monarch over the kingdom as a whole. This authority is endorsed by the cross, which symbolizes the divine right to rule. (We will see in a subsequent analysis of Peter Brook's film of *King Lear* how he introduces an orb in the opening scene.) Terry Hands had Richard, when forced to divest himself of the outward signs of his office, give the regalia to Bolingbroke, and almost frog march him to the throne:

> Now mark me how I will undo myself.
> I give this heavy weight from off my head,
> And this unwieldy sceptre from my hand,
> The pride of kingly sway from out my heart.
> With mine own tears I wash away my balm,
> With mine own hands I give away my crown
>
> (lines 202–7)

Bolingbroke was given the symbols that represented his temporal power and supposed spiritual authority, but instead of reinforcing his status, they were shown to undermine it: he simply didn't know how to handle them ... they looked unnatural and ill-fitting. David Suchet, now enthroned as Henry IV, orb in one hand, sceptre in the other, the crown on his head, made a startling contrast to the visual elegance and appropriateness of Alan Howard's portrayal of a monarch. Everything about the image of the new king clashed with that of the old, and the longer he persisted in the role the more powerfully mythical and golden the deposed king's image became. David Suchet's Bolingbroke was made to seem miscast for the role of king, and his unfamiliarity with the properties of kingship (the crown, orb and sceptre) made him appear even more awkward and like an imposter.

Another property was also used effectively in this production. The throne was presented as a dominating presence on the stage when Richard was still king, but was replaced by a desk after the deposition. The desk, unlike the throne, was not placed centre stage, but sited off-centre, as if to signal its occupant's reluctance to play a central dominating role in the theatre of the world. The new king sat behind it, his crown resting, not on his head, but on the desk beside him. The gorgeous golden robes of state favoured by his predecessor and worn with such aplomb, were replaced by more sober (and penitential) colours of purple and black.

What these examples demonstrate is the way in which properties can be used to *add* to the meaning of the play in performance. Active readers must consider them carefully, and always remember that the choice of a particular property needs to be argued for, and its role in the scene or the play as a whole, has to be thought through. However, there are times when a director or an actor chooses a property which results in a highly contentious reading of a scene, a character or even a whole play. As we have seen, Antony Sher decided to play the role of Richard III on titanium crutches. He also had his legs encased in callipers. The textual evidence for Richard's physical deformity is quite clear as he describes himself as 'deformed' and 'misshapen'. However, the extent to which an actor represents such physical deformity is open to argument. Laurence Olivier's Richard III had a slightly humped back, one shoulder was held higher than the other, and he walked with a pronounced limp. Antony Sher bounded around the stage with de-moniac energy, and was very soon using his crutches as weapons. In the wooing scene (I, ii) he used them to fight off Tressel who was attempting to protect Lady Anne, succeeding in stalking him around the stage and getting a huge laugh on 'Unmannered dog, stand thou where I command!' (the next three lines were cut). Later in the same scene, Sher succeeded in shocking the audience, himself, and not least, Penny Downie (Lady Anne), by 'slide[ing] one of the crutches under her skirt and between her legs' (*Year of the King*, p. 236). The problem for an audience watching such a bravura display is that it almost compels them to focus exclusively on the virtuoso skills of the actor. Antony Sher was rightly admired for his skill and courage in overcoming and mastering the handicap of having to move around a large stage on crutches, but, in reading the play, do we *want* to sympathize with, and admire Richard III? Is there not a danger that props such as the crutches and callipers will make Richard's disability a focus for sympathy, and, potentially, be seen as an *excuse* for what he does?

In both Laurence Olivier's film of the play, and Bill Alexander's stage production, it appears that Richard's handicap *is* intended, in some measure, to excuse him. That is, Richard's behaviour is caused by the fact that he is rejected by other people; a rejection based on an unfortunate accident of birth which has scarred him mentally, as well as physically. In such a reading of the play, Richard is *explained*: he is deformed by society (who reject him), and the moral responsibility for his actions is at least partially transferred on to others. The crutches signal that he is an outsider, a social outcast deserving as much of *pity* as of fear and loathing. Both Olivier and Antony Sher distanced their audiences further from Richard's actual responsibility for his actions by, as actors, and in Olivier's case, as director too, resolutely setting themselves against the presentation of an unsympathetic character. Both actors' reading of the part emphasized Richard as powerful, charismatic, sexy and witty, a reading which resists moral judgement. There is clearly no *right* reading of a Shakespeare text, but the argument concerning the fidelity of Olivier's and Antony Sher's text to Shakespeare's is that other readings are available. And in the case of the Olivier film, his directorial reading of the text required the suppression of textual evidence. Olivier cut the Queen Margaret role and, thus, Margaret's reading when she calls Richard a toad, and suggests that his deformity is the outward sign of an inner corruption (I, iii, line 246). But there is little room for questions of moral judgement in productions of *Richard III* which are seen by their directors as 'a comedy-thriller in the best sense of the words. Vintage Hitchcock, if you like' (*Year of the King*, p. 242).

Finally, before leaving the dramatic use of properties, I want to take a last look at what should be, by now, a familiar scene from *Richard III*. In Act One, scene two (the wooing scene between Richard and Lady Anne), I want to show that not only does the active reader need to acknowledge the presence and function of a particular property, but also, sometimes, to decide on its nature.

Towards the end of their dialogue, Richard apparently takes an extraordinary physical risk when he offers Anne,

> ... this sharp-pointed sword,
> Which if thou please to hide in this true breast
> And let the soul forth that adoreth thee,
> I lay it naked to the deadly stroke
> And humbly beg the death upon my knee.
>
> (I, ii, lines 174–8)

He then kneels and proceeds to admit his guilt in the murder of Anne's father-in-law and husband. If like Olivier and Sher we are looking at the scene in psychological terms we have to ask why she does not take the opportunity and immediately kill him? In Olivier's film it was obviously supposed to be because she had already fallen under the magnetic spell of this superman. The gesture, as performed by Olivier, merely indicates Richard's bravery and profound confidence in his own power. However, for Anne to seize the opportunity for revenge (she is observed young, highly vulnerable, alone, unsupported and a woman) is extremely hard, but, perhaps, not beyond the bounds of possibility. What might, in fact, happen (and does in my imaginary recreation of text-into-performance) to prevent her from killing Richard is the sword itself. The only description of the weapon comes from Richard. Although the stage directions indicate that it is a weapon belonging to him (*He lays his breast open. She offers at it with his sword*), there is nothing in the *words* to suggest that it has to belong to Richard. If the actor playing him were to move quickly and take a sword from the hands of one of the silent on-stage observers (say from Tressel or Berkeley), then the weapon might justifiably be a heavy two-handed sword. Obviously there is a great deal of difference between offering a young and slight girl a dagger, and giving her a sword almost as big as herself. I have seen the former result in Anne's striking at Richard and being restrained by his pinning her arm against the coffin. Encumbering her with a massive and unfamiliar weapon places her in a frustrating, confusing, and ultimately humiliating position. It is never a significant threat to Richard.

The choice in performance of the property concerned can, thus, show very different interpretations of the actions. If you decide the sword belongs to Richard, it is his personal weapon, light and, as he says, 'sharp-pointed', then you will emphasize in performance the magnitude of both the risks he takes and the extent of his personal charisma in having the confidence and the nerve to take it. But if the sword is heavy and cumbersome and belongs not to Richard but to one of the onlookers, a sword perhaps designed for ceremonial use, or for use by a professional soldier, Richard providing Anne with the weapon is shown as the action of a clever, calculating and totally cynical man.

As this example demonstrates, the choice of a property can be highly significant in manufacturing a particular meaning or meanings. A change in properties in this scene radically alters interpretation and makes it possible to question what has become the traditional audience response of admiration for Richard's virtuoso performance in seducing Anne. If an audience are made to see that there is no real physical risk involved for Richard, and that the 'victory' is hollow because the combatants were never remotely equal to begin with, then the view of the accomplished seducer and the foolish woman must be more difficult to sustain.

Sound Effects

> Be not afeared; the isle is full of noises,
> Sounds, and sweet airs, that give delight and hurt not.
> > (*The Tempest*, III, ii, lines 136–7)

It was probably the smouldering wadding from a cannon shot fired for effect during a performance of Shakespeare's *Henry VIII* in 1613 that set fire to the thatched roof of the first Globe theatre and resulted in the conflagration that destroyed it. As we have previously noted, the Elizabethan public theatres used all the available technology to assist them in their business of entertaining audiences. Ben Jonson, a contemporary of Shakespeare, and also, like him, a successful playwright, although one who appealed to a somewhat narrower audience, took time in the 1601 preface to an edition of his play *Everyman in his Humour* to satirize the then current fashion for elaborate stage effects brought about by primitive but effective stage machinery:

> He rather prays you will be pleased to see
> One such today as other plays should be;
> Where neither chorus wafts you o'er the seas,
> Nor creaking throne comes down the boys to please;
> Nor nimble squib is seen to make afeared
> The gentlewoman; not rolled bullet heard
> To say it thunders; nor tempestuous drum
> Rumbles to tell you when the storm doth come.
> > (quoted in *Elizabethan Popular Theatre*, p. 31)

Despite Jonson's objection, the use of the rolled bullet, and other methods of producing sound effects, kept the stage hands busy during performances of most Elizabethan and Jacobean plays. Almost all of the scenes in *Macbeth*, for example, require some kind of sound effect, ranging from the sound of thunder and drums, to the cry of women, horses' hoofs, hautboys, bells, owls, knocking, alarums, etc. A sound of a bell is used to great effect in the opening scene of *Hamlet*, both as a mark of time passing, as when Barnardo remarks, ''Tis now struck twelve. Get thee to bed, Francisco' (line 7), and also as a splendid and atmospheric cue for the first entry of the ghost of Hamlet's father.

BARNARDO
    Last night of all,
    When yond same star that's westward from the pole
    Had made his course t'illume that part of heaven
    Where now it burns, Marcellus and myself,
    The bell then beating one –
        Enter the Ghost
MARCELLUS
    Peace, break thee off. Look where it comes again.
                                    (lines 35–40)

Indeed, *Hamlet* only requires a minimum of the following sound cues: a cock crowing, ordnance firing, a bell striking one o'clock, crowds shouting/running etc., a funeral bell (for Ophelia's funeral), drums and cannon ('what warlike noise'). Sound effects, like properties, help in the creation of an appropriate mood and atmosphere; they can also be used to inform the audience (and the perceptive reader) of the significance of the action they are watching. For example, the sound of knocking on the doors of Macbeth's castle can sound quite horrific in the stillness of the night. At the beginning of the same play, the creation of the sound made by thunder prefigures the unrest and disturbance of the natural order that the subsequent action chronicles. The sound also proves the perfect background to the appearance of the 'black and midnight hags' and echoes the noise of the bloody battle taking place close by. The storm at sea encountered by Othello and Desdemona in *Othello* likewise prefigures in nature the schism that will wreck and finally destroy that marriage, and mad King Lear, in Act Three, scene two, of *King Lear*, throws back at the storm an inner tempest that rages in his mind, 'Blow, winds, and crack your cheeks! Rage! Blow!' (line 1).

Contemporary directors also sometimes make use of a particular sound effect to make a point about the play. For example, at the very beginning of Nicholas Hytner's production of *Measure for Measure* (RSC, 1988), before any words were spoken, the audience heard the amplified sound of a heavy steel door slamming shut whilst they watched the Duke, hesitatingly signing the statutes that will put so many of his subjects behind bars.

To sum up: nothing is ephemeral in a performance text. An individual sitting in the audience watching a play is continually working at making a synthesis of the many and varied signals being transmitted by the words spoken by the actors, the setting, the costumes, the gestures, the lighting and, not least, by the properties and sound effects. The active reader must also work towards such a synthesis and, in doing so, cannot afford to omit the use of properties and sound effects. Remember, you cannot single out and isolate any one signal generator and give it priority over the rest. An active reader must be aware of the interconnection of *everything* that is seen and heard in a text in performance in the mind's eye.

Shakespeare on Film

Although this book has, up to now, focused almost exclusively on the process of text into theatrical performance, most readers will be aware that there is an ever-increasing library of recorded performances of Shakespeare available on film and video. Indeed, the modern reader studying Shakespeare in the library or at home, is more likely to come to a play with a series of images derived from a previous filmed production in mind than from a theatrical performance. There is a long and interesting history of Shakespeare in the cinema that is well documented elsewhere, but, for the central issue that this book addresses – how literary texts are reconstructed into real or imagined theatrical performances – we need to acknowledge that the process of constructing text into recorded performance is a different, although related, process of making meanings.

Having access to a library of recordings of Shakespeare gives the student of text-into-performance a tremendous advantage, especially if that student has the material on video. Students watching a play in the theatre have no control over the performance. As we seem to have largely given up hissing and booing, let alone throwing rotten fruit, there are only two active ways left in which to respond: laughter/applause, or walking out. But performances on video offer the means through which the spectator *can* exert some measure of control over the product: he or she can interact positively and actively in the experience of watching performance. Instead of simply being a supplier to passive consumers of images and spoken language, the active reader can use the video medium to open up the processes through which meanings have been manufactured. The video recorder is the tool that can unlock the box. Unlike a film of a Shakespeare play shown on a conventional projector, a video can easily be stopped, the action frozen, and the composition of the frame analysed at leisure. A scene can be re-run as often as required, as well as being literally held up for attention. If the spectator intervenes in this way, and exercises control over the linear narrative, he or she can resist the narrative flow imposed by the illusionist techniques employed by almost all directors. However, it is no good having access to the technology if you have no idea how to use it effectively. How then should we use the facility we now have to examine performances of Shakespeare in such detail? Firstly, we are probably immediately aware that many of the aspects of theatrical art already explored in previous chapters are equally significant in recorded performances of Shakespeare: costume, properties, casting, setting, etc., all play a part in contextualizing the spoken text just as they do on the stage in a live performance. Secondly, however, we must acknowledge that there are significant differences between stage and screen, one of which is the power exercised by the film director over the reproduction of Shakespeare.

One of the inevitable problems associated with going to the theatre to see Shakespeare is that the interpretative power exercised by directors and designers over what is, essentially, a collective process, has tended to militate against the emergence in performance of a recognition of the plurality of meanings contained within the printed text. Audiences experiencing a performance of Shakespeare in the theatre are encouraged to accept that the particular (and inevitably partial) reading of the text that they have witnessed is definitive. Often, the theatrically manufactured perspectives of a text are so compelling as to preclude awareness of other possible readings: critical alternatives are not generally opened up by the experience of watching a performance. The classic example of this comes from a film of a Shakespeare play: Roman Polanski's *Macbeth*. Generations of unwary students have described the action of the camera in following Macbeth into Duncan's bedchamber as if it carried authorial as opposed to directorial authority. Of course, one of the tasks of a book such as this is to encourage students to challenge the apparent authority of the printed text, of theatrical and cinematic performances, and indeed the authority of all critical perspectives, including this one. However, the more authoritative the source of the text – the RSC, the National Theatre, the BBC, Penguin Books, Oxford or Cambridge University Press, etc., the more potentially difficult the task becomes. But, if the interpretative power of the theatre director to influence the way in which an audience understand a play is considerable, that of the film/television director is virtually absolute.

Although film and television are different media, both share a central characteristic that distinguishes their products from those of the live theatre: the lens of a camera is used to mediate the experience of watching performance because it is the camera, and not the spectator, which selects what it is that the viewer sees. A director uses it to construct the images, and the sequence of those images, that are eventually projected on to the screen. The dominant convention of movie making and editing (one that governs almost all film and television versions of Shakespeare) is designed to produce the illusion that the moving images the spectator is consuming are spontaneous and real, and not the products of a highly artificial, highly contrived medium. Almost all film and video versions of Shakespeare are constructed in such a way as to persuade the viewer that he or she is watching a 'coherent self-contained world portrayed as *unmediated* reality' (John Collick, *Shakespeare, Cinema and Society*, p. 82).

In a theatre, the eye of the spectator may well be drawn in a particular direction by grouping and/or an actor's performance. However, there is an element of choice and the spectator can choose to look elsewhere. Also, in the theatre, the audience is composed of individuals and groups who always see the action from different perspectives. Those seated in the front row of the stalls see a different performance from those occupying the back row of the upper gallery. Moreover, as we have seen, theatrical performances change over time; an actor's reading of a role will subtly evolve and certainly never be exactly the same from one performance to the next. In recorded performance the film's director, rather than the actor, decides where the focus should be. What the viewer sees and the way in which he or she sees it, has been carefully predetermined by the director. He or she chooses the camera angle, whether to use close-up, long shot, overhead shot or whatever, and therefore dictates not only what the audience will see, but also the *order* in which they will see it.

In selecting what an audience can see, the director also decides what they *cannot* see. A close-up of an actor or small group of actors may exclude others who could have been used to provide an alternative context. This is particularly significant in respect of the language of Shakespeare's dramas which, as we have seen, is essentially rhetorical: everything spoken was designed to be overheard by an audience and usually by actors on stage as well. All this is not simply a technical matter, it affects the way in which a film/video recording of a play is understood by an audience.

To give an example of how the camera regulates our perception of the final product, I want to briefly refer to a production from the BBC/ Time Life Shakespeare series. Many of the plays in this series are widely used in schools and colleges and one that probably receives more attention than most is Rodney Bennet's production of *Hamlet*, with Derek Jacobi in the title role. In common with most of the other productions in this series, the camera is used extensively to focus on small groups, individuals, and, especially, on head and shoulder shots. There is a widespread assumption in much of televised drama that the relatively small scale of the domestic television screen is best suited to close-ups. In almost all television drama the camera spends a high proportion of time focusing on the head, and, especially, on the eyes and mouth of individual characters. Bennet frequently uses his camera to observe the character speaking the text (especially Hamlet) rather than other characters listening and reacting to it. Consequently, as in the Olivier film of the play made some thirty years earlier and still widely screened, Bennet invites the viewer to 'read the faces', to look, as it were, behind the eyes of the characters and speculate on their psychology and personality, especially that of Hamlet. Just as Olivier prefaced his film with the statement 'this is the story of a man who could not make up his mind' and cut all the play's considerable political dimensions in order to focus exclusively on Hamlet, Rodney Bennet's camera, just as effectively, concentrates on the Prince's story largely to the exclusion of others. For example, one of the most dramatic scenes in *Hamlet* is the encounter between Hamlet and Ophelia immediately following the 'To be or not to be . . .' soliloquy (III, i). In a performance of the play on stage the audience will always be watching and aware of both performers (and perhaps, too, of the presence of Claudius and Polonius behind the arras) even though it is Hamlet who has most of the spoken text. In Rodney Bennet's production the camera focuses the viewer's attention almost exclusively on Hamlet. Although the presence of Ophelia is registered throughout the televising of the scene, the actress is usually filmed from behind, the camera looking over her shoulder towards Hamlet. The viewer, as a consequence, cannot see her full face. Even when her face is shown in close-up, it is in profile and the image blurred in order that the primary focus remains the Prince. Thus, consciously or not, the director makes Hamlet the subject of this scene. We watch, and are invited to share, *his* reactions to what is happening: he is the active, dynamic force; she is presented as passive. The scene thus constructed becomes almost exclusively a further extension of Hamlet's narrative, his crisis, his betrayal, whilst the betrayal of Ophelia by her father, is marginalized. This may at first seem acceptable, but *Hamlet* is concerned with more than Hamlet himself. There is the narrative of the Polonius family, the issues of the legitimate transfer of power, the threat of anarchy, and so on.

The camera is a wonderful tool in the hands of a good director. He or she can use it to tell an eloquent story without the use of any spoken text. Indeed, film and, although to a lesser extent, television too, is primarily a visual medium. This presents particular problems when a film is made of a Shakespeare play. Then tension arises between the demands of the language and the needs of the camera to find satisfying and eloquent images; the most successful films of Shakespeare manage to combine the two. What is vital for the active reader is that he or she should be aware of the conventions of the media of film and television and realize that, however seductive the images, a director is always trying to make the spectator look from a particular point of view; a point of view inevitably taken up as a result of an ideological position. For example, in Laurence Olivier's 1948 film of *Hamlet*, the camera is used highly skilfully and in a very mobile way to follow the progress of the Prince through a labyrinth set. It concentrates the viewer's attention on the action *from the point of view of Hamlet*. Deep-focus photography combined with the soaring and dipping of the camera produce a 'study of a tortured intellectual in which a great actor plays the part of a prince trapped in the labyrinth of his own mind' (*Shakespeare, Cinema and Society*, p. 63). Olivier's film becomes a study of one man's personality, but, at the expense of a considerable proportion of the play's content.

In a later film of the same play made, in 1963, by the Russian director Grigori Kozintsev, the camera is used to reject the romantic psychological introspection of Olivier's film. Kozintsev fills the screen with images that create a vivid social context for the play's narrative. Claudius is seen framed by armed guards; curious peasants are whipped away when they come too close to observing the funeral of Ophelia; Hamlet enters the castle on returning from Wittenberg and we witness the drawbridge being raised by a group of sweating men turning the capstan that operates it. Whatever Hamlet's concerns may be, there is always another world to whom they mean nothing. The castle, too, is not a metaphor for Hamlet's mind, but a real place, full of people and life, life that is shown in all its variety in order to put the events surrounding the death of Hamlet in some kind of social perspective.

Perhaps even more so than in the theatre, recorded performances of Shakespeare invite the spectator to appreciate the product as a seamless whole, and certainly not to look for the joins. But anyone who is interested in text-into-performance wants to know how and why some meanings are constructed and others neglected, as well as being ready to assert that some readings are legitimate whilst others are regarded as illegitimate. Kozintsev's films of *Hamlet* and *King Lear* are especially useful to the student of text-into-performance because the spoken language is Russian, translated and adapted for Kozintsev by Pasternak, and then turned into subtitles for English language screening. As a result, the spectator looks at and consciously reads the film's visual images with even more attention than usual.

Deconstructing a recorded performance can be difficult, but is always interesting. It is best to run the recording through at least once without stopping it so that, initially, you consume what you are meant to digest. Then be prepared to rerun it and to resist the almost inevitable driving momentum of the linear narrative. Always watch with a note pad and pencil to hand in order to register any particular moment of dramatic impact or obvious point of directorial interpretation. Watch with a friend, stopping the machine and possibly freezing a particular frame to discuss its composition.

It is impossible to reproduce in a book exactly the kind of visual analysis of a production of Shakespeare on video that I hope this chapter will encourage. I cannot adequately illustrate some of the central features of making meanings on film and video such as the juxtaposing of images, or the cutting from one shot to another. But, in an attempt to overcome these limitations, I have decided to illustrate some of the basic principles of 'reading' Shakespeare on film and video by referring to four productions of *King Lear*. (At least three of the four versions are widely available on video.)

King Lear on Video

Being able to compare contrasting productions of the same play is a highly enjoyable and constructive activity. In what follows, attention will be drawn to the director's use of the camera, his cutting and editing, costume, the grouping and composition of the image(s), properties and casting. All four directors start from the same point (a modern printed edition of *King Lear*), but, as you will see, they construct very different meanings.

Peter Brook

In 1971, Peter Brook made a film of the play (available on video) which had Paul Scofield as Lear. The film was largely shot on location in North Jutland, Denmark, during the winter of 1969. For Brook, the play seemed to revolve around the disjunction between Man and any notion of providence. He had previously staged the play at Stratford-upon-Avon (1962) and said, then, that 'Lear's society is primitive' and that the play constituted 'the prime example of the Theatre of the Absurd' (*The Shifting Point*, p. 62). For Brook, the central idea of the play seems to have been conveyed in the lines:

As flies to wanton boys, are we to the Gods;

They kill us for their sport.

(IV, i, 36–7)

He created a cruel, primitive and nihilistic world on film. It begins with a long tracking shot in which the camera moves in silence across a sea of faces over which the opening credits are superimposed. All the faces are male, all unsmiling, waiting and watching for something to happen. There is silence as the camera moves. These faces, we subsequently learn, are those of Lear's 100 knights. The focus then changes to reveal the interior of Lear's hut. A large phallic object (Lear's throne) is foregrounded with a seated semicircle of silent figures watching it intently. From the back wall comes the first sound and movement: a heavy door slamming shut. This sound of closure signals the opening of the spoken text: a text articulated not by Kent and Gloucester but, in close-up, by Paul Scofield's grizzled King. The camera is used in a close-up of Lear's face as Scofield, barely audible, and with little expression, speaks a highly truncated text.

In this opening scene, Brook's choice of two properties significantly contributed to stressing the harsh and primitive nature of Lear's kingdom. The Orb of State, passed by Kent to Goneril, is not a jewel-encrusted golden object readily associated with conventional and picturesque images of state pageantry, but a heavy crude metal object. It is passed from sister to sister, and, when it reaches Cordelia, her gesture clearly registers its bulk and weight as her outstretched hands dip when they feel its weight. The camera angle makes its dark shape (like a cloud) almost obscure Cordelia as she approaches to speak to Lear. Brook lends further emphasis to the primitive quality of this society through his decision to make the map, with which Lear literally, as well as symbolically, divides his kingdom, an area that seems to have been scored out of the ground and is covered by animal skins.

The costumes used in the film, while clearly from the distant past, are not readily associated with any particular historical period. They are largely free of ornamentation, strictly functional garments, as if their owners and makers had yet to acquire any sense of aesthetic values. Lear is dressed in animal skins, the huge feather collar of his robe giving him the appearance of an old vulture. His 100 knights display no signs of conventional heraldic pageantry; they, too, are dressed in animal skins. There is, literally, no colour in this world (Brook chose to film in black and white), nor is there any lyricism; the only hint of that comes in the figure of Cordelia, who, at a point in the opening scene, is filmed briefly from behind, a shot that shows her long black hair swept back from her face and held at the back by a simple leather grip before flowing down her back suggesting the graceful lines of a Viking long-boat.

The final images of the opening sequence showed Lear storming out of his chamber. The camera emphasized his enormous bulk, stressing his physical dominance over the expectant faces awaiting him – the 100 knights. The composition of this, and similar images at the opening of the action, plus the casting of Paul Scofield, an actor in reality well below Lear's stated age of 'Fourscore and upward', illustrates a man far from his dotage; still powerful, strong and threatening. The whole of this opening sequence emphasizes the harshness of this world, the close-ness of men to animals, the almost entire absence of any human warmth, and, above all, the lowering presence and unpredictable power of Sco-field's King Lear.

Grigori Kozintsev

Kozintsev's film (made in Russia in 1970), also charts the progress of a King from power to powerlessness. However, unlike Brook, who sees Lear's world as absurd, that is, lacking in ultimate meaning, Kozintsev is intent to show that whether or not the actions have ultimate meaning, what happens to King Lear and his immediate family *does* have an effect (and a meaning) that extends far beyond the confines of the history of Lear's personal misery. His intention is to move beyond the traditional focus on the character of the King himself in order to explore wider issues.

The opening sequence of Kozintsev's film (also shot in black and white) is a highly emotive series of images. It opens by showing groups of ragged people moving slowly and with difficulty through a barren and hostile landscape. No one speaks. The camera moves in to focus on individuals, including a couple pushing a sleeping (or dead) child on a barrow. The spectator sees the feet of the walkers, toes protruding from boots barely holding together. These are peasants, refugees, perhaps hunted, certainly dispossessed. The Russian audience who first saw this film, and for many of whom the memory of suffering brought about by the war with Nazi Germany was still green, would doubtless have had no difficulty in identifying with them. The camera discloses that the army of the dispossessed are moving towards a huge fortress: Lear's Castle. The building's massive walls and the sheer scale of the place in the empty landscape offers the viewer a forceful metaphor of power.

The camera eventually takes us inside the walls and shows us more of the people who make up the society ruled by this king. This is a very real place; it feels located in history, not part of some distant and mythologized past. The pictures of ordinary people remind the spectator that the division of the kingdom will have repercussions not only for Lear and his daughters, but also for the vast majority of innocent observers who will subsequently be drawn into war. Indeed, some of the most telling images from the film illustrate the shattering effects of the conflict upon ordinary people.

The opening minutes of Kozintsev's film introduce the spectator to the hierarchy of this society. First, we are shown the poor outside the fortress. Then, inside the walls, we see soldiers and servants. Finally, inside a room within the building we are shown those with power: the aristocracy or ruling élite surrounding King Lear. However, whereas Brook's camera makes Lear's character and personality the subject for scrutiny (in the opening minutes the camera concentrates almost entirely upon him, and there are lengthy close-ups of Scofield's face), Kozintsev's exposition largely ignores the King, preferring instead to prefigure the breadth of suffering that will result from his division of the kingdom by showing the people who will be affected by it. In Brook's version the King is the first to speak, first to appear in close-up; in Kozintsev's film as in the play itself his appearance is delayed. Only after establishing the social context of the subsequent action, and after Gloucester and Kent have begun to speak the opening text (cut entirely in Brook's version), is the focus changed to the King. The camera is prompted by the sound of tinkling bells and laughter to shift the attention on to a small, low door set into the wall of the chamber. Suddenly the door is opened and Lear emerges. Kozintsev gives his actor a useful property at this point: the fool's mask, which he holds briefly in front of his face before, almost reluctantly, leaving his private world to negotiate that of the public chamber. Whilst the opening sequence has shown people gravitating towards this, the seat of power, and others waiting for the King to exercise that power, Lear, Kozintsev suggests, has literally been playing the fool.

Costume has been used to indicate the social hierarchy, and, in the case of Lear's first appearance, his disregard of the social conventions governing his role as king (he is dressed in a shapeless plain robe, with none of the conventional trappings of a king). It is also used to emphasize that this society is ultimately governed by force. The many shots of soldiers stress their power (they are on horseback and armed), as opposed to the peasants, who are powerless; vulnerable both to man-made and natural disasters. These people are those, Kozintsev seems to suggest, of whom King Lear has taken too little care.

Watching Kozintsev's work, the viewer is left in little doubt as to the reality of Lear's power. The world he inhabits, and whose innocent citizens his actions radically affect, are painstakingly re-created on screen. This is not a mythical place, but a political world, soon to be sent reeling under the effects of unbridled power.

Michael Elliott and Laurence Olivier

Our third example of a production of the play begins on almost a diametrically opposite note. Michael Elliott's production for Granada Television (1983) opens the action with a setting designed to recall Stonehenge, suggesting an ancient Britain redolent with vague but powerful Druidical mythology. The production is also concerned with a then living legend: as the opening titles suggest, the audience are prepared not only for the appearance of King Lear, but also for the actor chosen to represent him: Laurence Olivier. They tell the viewer that it is not Granada Television, but 'Laurence Olivier' who 'presents' *King Lear*.

Unlike the previous two versions, this production was made in colour. In the opening shots the use of colour in the costumes emphasized a rich court, displaying a somewhat vague historical costume midway between ancient Britain and the Middle Ages. There is no lengthy exposition such as that used by Kozintsev; neither is the text cut as in the Brook version. Kent and Gloucester begin the action with their conversation in front of the 'stones'. It is not long, however, before the entrance of Lear is signalled; it has all the hallmarks of that reserved for 'star' actors. The sound of muted trumpets is heard, from the rear of the set emerge, first, the immediate family of the King, and, then, from out of the light projected on to the rear cyclorama, comes the figure of Lear, leaning on Cordelia, preceded by a man carrying a ceremonial sword. When he is seated, all the other characters throw themselves to the ground in a collective gesture of homage.

A crucial property required in the first scene is the map of Lear's kingdom. We noted that in Brook's film it emphasized the fundamentally primitive nature of the society. In Kozintsev's version it is literally (and symbolically) torn apart by the King's rage. But here, the map is a vast and colourful picture, resembling a giant rug. Seen from one of the many overhead shots used in this production, it resembles a map of the British Isles seen through the eyes of the Middle Ages. The effect is decorative and pictorial, adding to the overall spectacle of Elliott's staging of the opening of the play. There is none of the bleakness and pessimism of Brook's opening shots, nor is there any attempt to provide a wider political context for the action, as in the work of Kozintsev. This opening series of images presents a traditional conservative reading of the text that focuses upon the *character* of the King himself, and the mercurial nature of his personality. Ultimately it invites our sympathy for one 'more sinn'd against than sinning' (III, ii, lines 58–9).

Jonathan Miller

Finally, I come to Jonathan Miller's direction of *King Lear* for the BBC/Time Life Shakespeare series, transmitted in 1982. Miller's production opens without any ceremony. Unlike Olivier's entrance, where the assembled Court prostrate themselves on the ground in front of him, Hordern bustles into the picture, almost unnoticed. The setting is small and enclosed, resembling the interior of a domestic house. The only items of furniture used are a table and chair. Miller chooses to emphasize, not the ritual quality of the occasion, nor the fact that the King is transacting momentous affairs of state, but, through his selection of properties, costume and casting, he urges the viewer to accept that this is to be an essentially domestic tragedy, based around the story of a family in crisis.

Through his focus on the domestic microcosm of family life Miller hoped to make a telling connection between it, and the macrocosm of the state itself: '*King Lear* seems to show how families fall apart when parents abdicate their responsibility and their powers, and how the state similarly fragments if its symbolic head abdicates responsibility' (*Subsequent Performances*, p. 131). Miller chose a map for Lear's division of the kingdom that was small, plain and easily displayed – it could easily be a will. The table on which it was placed was simple, and of domestic proportions. On occasions other than this, he seems to suggest, it would have been the focus for the family gathering to share a meal. The costumes worn by the actors were those made for daily living rather than for state occasions, and Miller located the action in historical time (Jacobean England), rather than associating it with some mythical Druidical antiquity.

Miller used the camera in a skilful painterly way to frame the action so as to emphasize the family groupings. For example, when Lear begins to divide the kingdom, the camera invariably uses deep focus in order to show not only Lear, but also the reactions to what he is saying of his three daughters, their husbands and suitors. These family groups often echo seventeenth-century genre paintings, again emphasizing Miller's conviction that the play, for all its pagan invocations, was really concerned with issues affecting the original audience of Stuart England. Finally, by casting Michael Hordern as King Lear, Miller set the seal on his family drama, for Hordern, almost uniquely amongst British actors, has cornered the market in the portrayal of warm, avuncular figures (his is the voice used for Paddington Bear cartoons).

This kind of exercise demonstrates that the range of meanings which arise through combining study of printed texts with video versions of Shakespeare's plays are greatly increased by using a record of more than one performance. But, the active reader of Shakespeare cannot productively make use of such material unless he or she is able to critically assess it in the light of his or her own reading of the printed text. Nothing can replace the act of reading, you cannot substitute the experience of watching a play for the experience of reading it. However, the experience of both will be enriched if they are made to comment and reflect on one another.

The bibliography will guide you towards some of the commercially available video recordings of Shakespeare. From time to time Shakespeare's plays are screened on television and there is nothing to prevent you from taping them for your own private study. For example, in 1989, the BBC transmitted a recording of a production of *Othello* from the Market Theatre in Johannesburg, South Africa. This powerful production, in which Othello is played by a black actor, makes a wonderful contrast to other productions of the play produced in very different political circumstances such as Olivier's *Othello*, and that made for the BBC/Time Life series.

The library of Shakespeare on video that now exists is constantly expanding and provides an excellent source of material to help you make your own imaginative performances, but, video cannot entirely replace the experience of live performance. Wherever you watch performances of Shakespeare, remember that you ought not to automatically surrender yourself to someone else's view of Shakespeare's world. Don't leave your intellect along with your coat in the theatre cloakroom, and don't let the flickering light from the television screen shift your brain into neutral. If you can deconstruct at least part of what directors, actors and designers have painstakingly constructed, you will draw attention not only to how and why meanings are manufactured, but also to the inescapable fact that texts in performance can only contain a limited number of ideas, while written versions potentially retain them all. For this reason, it is important to be both an active reader and an active spectator. Your pleasure in texts and performances will increase tremendously when you can both construct and deconstruct productions for yourself.

Select Bibliography

BARTON, JOHN, *Playing Shakespeare* (Methuen, 1984)

BERRY, RALPH (ed.), *On Directing Shakespeare* (Hamish Hamilton, 1989)

BEVINGTON, DAVID, *Action is Eloquence: Shakespeare's Language of Gesture* (Harvard University Press, 1984)

Tudor Drama and Politics: A Critical Approach to Topical Meaning (Harvard University Press, 1968)

BROCKBANK, PHILIP (ed.), *Players of Shakespeare, Vol. I* (CUP, 1988)

BROOK, PETER, *The Shifting Point: Forty Years of Theatrical Exploration, 1946–87* (Methuen, 1989)

The Empty Space (Penguin Books, 1972)

CALLOW, SIMON, *Being an Actor* (Methuen, 1984)

COLLICK, JOHN, *Shakespeare, Cinema and Society* (Manchester University Press, 1989)

COOK, JUDITH, *Directors' Theatre: Sixteen Leading Theatre Directors on the State of Theatre in Britain Today* (Hodder and Stoughton, 1989)

DAVIES, ANTHONY, *Filming Shakespeare's Plays* (CUP, 1988)

DESSEN, ALAN, *Elizabethan Stage Conventions and Modern Interpreters* (CUP, 1986)

DONALDSON, PETER, *Shakespearean Films/Shakespearean Directors* (Unwin Hyman, 1990)

DURBACH, ERROL (ed.), *Essays in Celebration of the 150th Anniversary of Henrik Ibsen's Birth* (Macmillan, 1980)

GASKILL, WILLIAM, *A Sense of Direction* (Faber and Faber, 1988)

GOODWIN, JOHN (ed.), *Peter Hall's Diaries* (Hamish Hamilton, 1983)

GURR, ANDREW, *The Shakespearean Stage, 1574–1642* (CUP, 1982)

HATTAWAY, MICHAEL, *Elizabethan Popular Theatre: Plays in Performance* (Routledge, 1985)

JACKSON, R. and SMALLWOOD, R. (eds.), *Players of Shakespeare, Vol. II* (CUP, 1988)

MARSHALL, NORMAN, *The Producer and the Play* (Macdonald, 1957)

MILLER, JONATHAN, *Subsequent Performances* (Faber and Faber, 1986)

OLIVIER, LAURENCE, *On Acting* (Sceptre, 1984)

RUTTER, CAROL, *Clamorous Voices: Shakespeare's Women Today* (Women's Press, 1988)

SALGADO, GAMINI (ed.), *Eyewitnesses of Shakespeare: Firsthand Accounts of Performances, 1590–1890* (Sussex University Press, 1975)

SHER, ANTONY, *Year of the King: An Actor's Diary* (Chatto and Windus, 1985)

SLATER, ANN PASTERNAK, *Shakespeare the Director* (Harvester Press, 1984)

THOMSON, PETER, *Shakespeare's Theatre* (Routledge, 1983)

A list of BBC productions that are currently on sale to the general public can be obtained from:

> BBC Television Enterprises
> Education and Training Sales
> London W12 0TT

An invaluable list of *all* the available audio-visual material concerning Shakespeare (including productions on film and video) can be obtained from:

> BUFVC
> Greek Street
> London W1 5LR
> Tel. 071 734 3687

It is published by the British Universities Film and Video Council and costs (1990) £5.00 for members and £9.50 for non-members. The price includes UK postage.

FOR THE BEST IN PAPERBACKS, LOOK FOR THE 🐧

In every corner of the world, on every subject under the sun, Penguin represents quality and variety – the very best in publishing today.

For complete information about books available from Penguin – including Puffins, Penguin Classics and Arkana – and how to order them, write to us at the appropriate address below. Please note that for copyright reasons the selection of books varies from country to country.

In the United Kingdom: Please write to *Dept E.P., Penguin Books Ltd, Harmondsworth, Middlesex, UB7 0DA.*

If you have any difficulty in obtaining a title, please send your order with the correct money, plus ten per cent for postage and packaging, to *PO Box No 11, West Drayton, Middlesex*

In the United States: Please write to *Dept BA, Penguin, 299 Murray Hill Parkway, East Rutherford, New Jersey 07073*

In Canada: Please write to *Penguin Books Canada Ltd, 2801 John Street, Markham, Ontario L3R 1B4*

In Australia: Please write to the *Marketing Department, Penguin Books Australia Ltd, P.O. Box 257, Ringwood, Victoria 3134*

In New Zealand: Please write to the *Marketing Department, Penguin Books (NZ) Ltd, Private Bag, Takapuna, Auckland 9*

In India: Please write to *Penguin Overseas Ltd, 706 Eros Apartments, 56 Nehru Place, New Delhi, 110019*

In the Netherlands: Please write to *Penguin Books Netherlands B.V., Postbus 195, NL–1380AD Weesp*

In West Germany: Please write to *Penguin Books Ltd, Friedrichstrasse 10–12, D–6000 Frankfurt/Main 1*

In Spain: Please write to *Alhambra Longman S.A., Fernandez de la Hoz 9, E–28010 Madrid*

In Italy: Please write to *Penguin Italia s.r.l., Via Como 4, I-20096 Pioltello (Milano)*

In France: Please write to *Penguin Books Ltd, 39 Rue de Montmorency, F-75003 Paris*

In Japan: Please write to *Longman Penguin Japan Co Ltd, Yamaguchi Building, 2-12-9 Kanda Jimbocho, Chiyoda-Ku, Tokyo 101*

PENGUIN LITERARY CRITICISM

A Lover's Discourse   Roland Barthes

'*A Lover's Discourse* ... may be the most detailed, painstaking anatomy of desire we are ever likely to see or need again ... The book is an ecstatic celebration of love and language and ... readers interested in either or both ... will enjoy savouring its rich and dark delights' – *Washington Post Book World*

The New Pelican Guide to English Literature   Boris Ford (ed.)

The indispensable critical guide to English and American literature in nine volumes, erudite yet accessible. From the ages of Chaucer and Shakespeare, via Georgian satirists and Victorian social critics, to the leading writers of the 1980s, all literary life is here.

The Theatre of the Absurd   Martin Esslin

This classic study of the dramatists of the Absurd examines the origins, nature and future of a movement whose significance has transcended the bounds of the stage and influenced the whole intellectual climate of our time.

The Theory of the Modern Stage   Eric Bentley (ed.)

In this anthology Artaud, Brecht, Stanislavski and other great theatrical theorists reveal the ideas underlying their productions and point to the possibilities of the modern theatre.

Introducing Shakespeare   G. B. Harrison

An excellent popular introduction to Shakespeare – the legend, the (tantalizingly ill-recorded) life and the work – in the context of his times: theatrical rivalry, literary piracy, the famous performance of *Richard II* in support of Essex, and the fire which finally destroyed the Globe.

Aspects of the Novel   E. M. Forster

'I say that I have never met this kind of perspicacity in literary criticism before. I could quote scores of examples of startling excellence' – Arnold Bennett. Originating in a course of lectures given at Cambridge, *Aspects of the Novel* is full of E. M. Forster's habitual wit, wisdom and freshness of approach.

FOR THE BEST IN PAPERBACKS, LOOK FOR THE 🐧

PENGUIN SELF-STARTERS

Self-Starters are designed to help you develop skills and proficiency in the subject of your choice. Each book has been written by an expert and is suitable for school-leavers, students, those considering changing their career in mid-stream and all those who study at home.

Titles published or in preparation:

FOR THE BEST IN PAPERBACKS, LOOK FOR THE 🐧

PENGUIN CRITICAL STUDIES

Described by *The Times Educational Supplement* as 'admirable' and 'superb', Penguin Critical Studies is a specially developed series of critical essays on the major works of literature for use by students in universities, colleges and schools.

titles published or in preparation include:

SHAKESPEARE
Antony and Cleopatra
As You Like It
Hamlet
Julius Caesar
King Lear
Measure for Measure
A Midsummer Night's Dream
Much Ado About Nothing
Othello
Romeo and Juliet
Shakespeare's History Plays
Shakespeare – Text into Performance
The Tempest
Troilus and Cressida
The Winter's Tale

CHAUCER
Chaucer
The Nun's Priest's Tale
The Pardoner's Tale
The Prologue to the Canterbury
   Tales

FOR THE BEST IN PAPERBACKS, LOOK FOR THE 🐧

PENGUIN CRITICAL STUDIES

Described by *The Times Educational Supplement* as 'admirable' and 'superb', Penguin Critical Studies is a specially developed series of critical essays on the major works of literature for use by students in universities, colleges and schools.

titles published or in preparation include:

William Blake
The Changeling
Doctor Faustus
Emma *and* Persuasion
Great Expectations
The Great Gatsby
Heart of Darkness
The Poetry of Gerard
   Manley Hopkins
Joseph Andrews
Mansfield Park
Middlemarch
The Mill on the Floss
Nostromo
Paradise Lost

The Poetry of Alexander Pope
The Portrait of a Lady
A Portrait of the Artist as a
   Young Man
The Return of the Native
Rosencrantz and Guildenstern
   are Dead
Sons and Lovers
Tennyson
Tess of the D'Urbervilles
To the Lighthouse
The Waste Land
Wordsworth
Wuthering Heights
Yeats